Stainton Moses

Psychography

A Treatise on one of the Objective Forms of Psychic or Spiritual Phenomena

Stainton Moses

Psychography

A Treatise on one of the Objective Forms of Psychic or Spiritual Phenomena

ISBN/EAN: 9783337425302

Printed in Europe, USA, Canada, Australia, Japan

Cover: Foto ©Lupo / pixelio.de

More available books at **www.hansebooks.com**

PSYCHOGRAPHY:

A TREATISE

ON ONE OF THE OBJECTIVE FORMS

OF

PSYCHIC OR SPIRITUAL PHENOMENA.

By "M. A. (OXON.)"

1878.

LONDON: W. H. HARRISON, 38 GREAT RUSSELL STREET.

A testimony is sufficient when it rests on—

1. A great number of sensible witnesses, who agree on having seen clearly.
2. Who are sane, bodily and mentally.
3. Who are impartial and disinterested.
4. Who unanimously agree.
5. Who solemnly certify to the fact.

VOLTAIRE,
(Philosophical Dictionary).

"Never utter these words: 'I do not know this; therefore it is false.'"

"One must study to know, know to understand, understand to judge."

NARADA,
(Hindû Philosopher).

PREFACE.

The following pages are concerned with what has been variously called Independent, Direct, or Spirit Writing. I have ventured to call it PSYCHOGRAPHY, a term intelligible in itself, moulded on already existing words, and expressive of what clumsy periphrases have hitherto vaguely conveyed.

I was under the impression, when I first applied the term, that it was as new to the subject as it certainly was to me. I find, however, that I am using a word which has been before applied; and I am not sorry that I am only giving extended use to a term which is obviously applicable and convenient.

My object has been to present within convenient space a record of facts bearing on one form only of Psychic Phenomena. To this end I have cut out from the quoted records all that bore upon other phenomena not now under consideration.

I have desired to present no theory for acceptance. I have, indeed, enumerated several, and have shown in some cases how far they do or do not square with observed facts. But I have never presumed to take upon myself the office of advocate of any. So far have I kept myself from this that I have, in some cases, ventured to excise expressions of opinion from quoted records, where it was possible to do so without doing any violence to the context.

In submitting what I have written to the judgment of my readers, I profess my own firm belief in the trustworthy nature of the facts recorded, and my own profound sense of their far-reaching importance, both on grounds of their intrinsic value, and as parts of a great system of Psychological Fact and Phenomenon, the study of which must eventually throw a flood of light on some of the problems that, in the present day, are at once most interesting and most perplexing.

That men of trained and practised intellect should be found willing to devote the assiduous labour of a long life to some minute subject, in the hope of clearing up one small phase of it, is, from one point of view, a hopeful and encouraging fact; but it tends to engender thoughts the reverse of cheerful, when we reflect that this very search after truth in one of its minute phases is frequently allied to a scornful contempt for that noblest study of humanity, Man's own Nature, Powers, and Destiny.

The result, primarily, of ignorance, next of prejudice, finally of disgust at oft-detected fraud, this attitude—this unworthy attitude—can, I believe, better be combated by patient exposition of the truth than by any proselytizing, however vigorous and wide-spread, or by any controversy, however skilfully conducted. A Fact must finally drop into its place; it matters not much, save to those who might profit by knowledge of it, whether now or in a succeeding age, when our children will, it is to be hoped, be wiser than their fathers.

It is with this conviction that I have endeavoured to elucidate one among many of the facts which testify to the existence of a soul in man, and to its independent action beyond his physical body; an earnest of its survival and independent life when released by death from its earthly prison-house.

M. A. (Oxon.)

SYNOPSIS OF CONTENTS.

	PAGE
PREFACE,	5
LIST OF WORKS BEARING ON THE SUBJECT,	11
INTRODUCTION,	13
PSYCHOGRAPHY IN THE PAST: GULDENSTUBBÉ—CROOKES,	19
PERSONAL EXPERIENCES IN PRIVATE, AND WITH PUBLIC PSYCHICS,	25

GENERAL CORROBORATIVE EVIDENCE.

I. THAT ATTESTED BY THE SENSES—

1. Of Sight.

Evidence of Mr. E. T. Bennett,	33
,, a Malvern Reporter,	35
,, Mr. James Burns,	36
,, Mr. H. D. Jencken,	38

2. Of Hearing.

Evidence of Mr. Serjeant Cox,	41
,, Mr. George King,	44
,, Mr. Hensleigh Wedgwood,	49
,, Miss * * *	50
,, Canon Mouls,	52

8 *Synopsis of Contents.*

	PAGE
Evidence of Baroness Von Vay,	52
,, G. H. Adshead,	53
,, W. P. Adshead,	53
,, E. H. Valter,	54
,, J. L. O'Sullivan,	58
,, Epes Sargent,	60
,, James O. Sargent,	63
,, John Wetherbee,	65
,, H. B. Storer,	66
,, C. A. Greenleaf,	66
,, Public Committee with Watkins,	67

II. FROM THE WRITING OF LANGUAGES UNKNOWN TO THE PSYCHIC.

Ancient Greek—Evidence of Hon. R. Dale Owen and Mr. Blackburn. (Slade),	71
Dutch, German, French, Spanish, Portuguese. (Slade),	78
Russian—Evidence of Madame Blavatsky. (Watkins),	78
Romaic—Evidence of T. T. Timayenis. (Watkins),	79
Chinese. (Watkins),	79

III. FROM SPECIAL TESTS WHICH PRECLUDE PREVIOUS PREPARATION OF THE WRITING.

Psychics and Conjurers Contrasted,	80
Slade before the Research Committee of the British National Association of Spiritualists,	83
Slade Tested by C. Carter Blake, Doc. Sci.,	90
Evidence of Rev. J. Page Hopps. (Slade),	94
,, W. H. Harrison. (Slade),	96
,, J. Seaman. (Slade),	98

Synopsis of Contents.

	PAGE
WRITING within Slates securely screwed together. Evidence of Mrs. Andrews and J. Mould,	101
DICTATION of Words at the Time of the Experiment.	
Evidence of A. R. Wallace, F.R.G.S.,	104
,, Hensleigh Wedgwood, J.P.,	105
,, Rev. Thomas Colley,	106
,, W. Oxley,	106
,, George Wyld, M.D.,	108
,, Miss Kislingbury,	109
WRITING in Answer to Questions Inside a Closed Box. Evidence of Messrs. Adshead,	113
STATEMENT of Circumstances under which Experiments with F. W. Monck were conducted at Keighley,	119
WRITING on Glass Coated with White Paint. Evidence of Benjamin Coleman,	120
LETTERS ADDRESSED TO "THE TIMES" ON THE SUBJECT OF THE PROSECUTION OF HENRY SLADE BY MESSRS. JOY, JOAD, AND PROFESSOR BARRETT, F.R.S.E.,	121
EVIDENCE OF W. H. HARRISON, EDITOR OF "THE SPIRITUALIST,"	125
SUMMARY OF FACTS NARRATED,	127

DEDUCTIONS, EXPLANATIONS, AND THEORIES.

THE NATURE OF THE FORCE: ITS MODE OF OPERATION.

Evidence of C. Carter Blake, Doc. Sci., and Conrad Cooke, C.E., ... 128

Synopsis of Contents.

DETONATING NOISES IN CONNEXION WITH IT.

    Evidence of Hensleigh Wedgwood, J. Page Hopps, Thomas Colley, ... 133

METHOD OF DIRECTION OF THE FORCE.

    Dr. Collyer's Theory, ... 135
    Dr. George Wyld's Theory, ... 140
    The Occultist's Theory, ... 141
    The Spiritualist's Theory, ... 145

APPENDIX.

The Berlin Court Conjurer on Slade, ... 149
Slade with the Grand Duke Constantine, ... 150
Recent Experiment with Monck, ... 151

LIST OF BOOKS BEARING ON PSYCHOGRAPHY AND SUBJECTS OF A KINDRED NATURE.

La Réalité des Esprits et le Phénomène Merveilleux de leur Écriture Directe. Baron L. de Guldenstubbé.

Primitive Christianity and Modern Spiritualism. Eugene Crowell, M.D.

Planchette. Epes Sargent.

Experimental Investigation of the Spirit Manifestations. Robert Hare, M.D.

Miracles and Modern Spiritualism. A. R. Wallace, F.R.G.S.

Researches in the Phenomena of Spiritualism. W. Crookes, F.R.S.

Report on Spiritualism of the Committee of the London Dialectical Society.

Arcana of Spiritualism. Hudson Tuttle.

Letters and Tracts on Spiritualism. Judge Edmonds.

Isis Unveiled. H. P. Blavatsky.

The Debatable Land.
Footfalls on the Boundary of Another World. } Hon. R. Dale Owen.

*** These Books can all be obtained from the Publisher of this volume.

INTRODUCTION.

BEFORE commencing the special work which I have set myself to do, I wish to make clear what I propose and what I do not propose to attempt in its execution.

I propose, then, to set forth certain facts within my own knowledge respecting one class of Psychic Phenomena—viz., Psychography, or Abnormal Writing. These facts (respecting a subject which obtained much publicity during the past year) I set forth on my own authority, and as part of my own experience in the investigation of Psychic Phenomena.

I propose, further, to record, in a convenient form for reference, certain other facts of a similar nature testified to by others. In doing so, I shall rigidly adhere to the special fact under notice, and shall eliminate all evidence that will not bear rigid scrutiny. Confining myself to this one class of phenomena, I shall avoid repetition and the needless multiplication of records. Fully conscious that evidence of this nature is cumulative, I also believe that there is a point beyond which the cumulative power ceases, and I judge it best to narrow down the issue as far as possible.

Respecting these facts, I do not propose to maintain any theory, though I shall briefly enumerate some hypotheses which are put forward. I shall not vex myself and perplex my readers by the discussion of any *à priori* grounds of rejection with which some investigators bewilder themselves. I have nothing to do with the allegation that such and such things are *ex rerum naturâ*, and so are to be rejected without the formality of a trial. This is an ancient method—more antique than venerable—of disposing of new facts. There was a time, somewhere in the world's history, when it was employed to burke almost every manifestation of truth which was new and unwelcome, just as there comes a time in the history of each new discovery when the old method is abandoned, and those who have employed it endeavour, with a shame-faced smile, to show that they were only joking after all, and were, though we might not have observed it, truth's best and truest friends.

I do not propose to anticipate that time in the history of these Psychic Phenomena by any premature argument. Convinced that the time is near at hand when Science will recognise her duty in this respect, I will patiently wait for the time when some of its prominent representatives will abandon a false position with such grace as they may.

As to the facts, I shall not attempt to maintain anything more than that they furnish evidence of the existence of a Force, and of a governing Intelligence external to a human body. That Force is conveniently called Psychic, and is the Odic, or Od Force, of Reichenbach; the Nerve Force, or Aura, of other writers; the Ectenic Force of Thury; the Akasa of the Hindû; or, comprehensively, Vital Force. The name matters little; but the term Psychic and its compounds, as applied to the Force, to the channel through which it flows, and to its various forms of manifestation, seems most simple and free from objection.*

I do not propose to burden my record with any arguments as to the source and character of the Intelligence, except where such are plain deductions from my narrative.

I will not enter into any disquisition on the use of the terms Soul and Spirit. I do not care which is used, though, for myself, I employ the term Spirit as equivalent to what St. Paul called the Spiritual Body as opposed to the Physical Body. Soul I consider to be the Divine Principle by virtue of possession of which man is an heir of Immortality. Others use the terms differently, making the Soul to be the Astral or Spiritual Body, and the Spirit the equivalent of what I call Soul. This is not the place for argument on this point. By the use of either term I intend to indicate the Spiritual Principle in man—the Self, the *Ego*, the Inner Being—which, acting through the material frame, is, as I believe, independent in its existence, and will survive the death of the body.

Respecting this Intelligence which is displayed in the messages written out by these abnormal means, I

---

* It is usual among many who record these phenomena to employ the term *Medium* for the *Psychic*, and from it to fabricate such philologically barbarous words as *mediumistic*. The terms will be found in use in many of the published records; but I have employed the term Psychic and its compounds, as, in my judgment, preferable.

will not maintain that it is or is not worthy of attention on account of the matter of its communications. I could say something on the just lines of criticism in this respect, but my purpose is served without any opening of side issues. What is written may be as foolish as my critic pleases. If it be never so silly, it will serve for my argument. Is it written at all? Then let us leave its nonsense alone, and account for its presence as a fact.

Nor will I maintain that the messages always, or even generally, proceed from the source pretended. No more fruitful source of controversy has arisen than this. Taste and sense of decorum and propriety are outraged by the claim that is made for these frequently silly and ludicrous writings, that they proceed from the source alleged, which, as often as not, is some relative of the experimenter's or some great and illustrious name in history. The shock to good taste and feeling so administered puts the investigator into an attitude of indignant opposition. He refuses to credit what is to him so monstrous, and jumps, in anger, to the conclusion that what is improbable in the explanation extends also to the fact. I trust that any who do me the honour to read what I write will allow me to pin their attention to the bare fact, and to ask them to leave the matter of the writing to another time. Just now, I will say nothing whatever about the contents. It is sufficient that they are in evidence as an objective fact.

I will not maintain that the Intelligence is always independent of that of the Psychic in whose presence these phenomena occur, or of some or all of the persons present. This is not the place in which to discuss the powers of the human spirit, or the limits of its trans-corporeal action.

I will not even maintain that the Intelligence is *intelligent*. Sometimes it is not; but always, so far as I know, there is evidence of plan, of design, of purpose. I will not go so far, either, as to discuss the question whether, in given cases, the Intelligence is human or sub-human. These are all points which merit grave discussion, and on each of which I could say much, were it not for the fear of diverting attention from my one point—the fact of Psychography. In this connexion I may, however, quote the conclusion arrived at by Mr. Crookes, F.R.S., after a long series of scientific experiments and observations, recorded in the *Quarterly Journal of Science*, January, 1874. Speaking of the Phenomena of Percussive Sounds, he says:—

An important question here forces itself upon the attention. *Are the movements and sounds governed by intelligence?* At a very early stage of the inquiry, it was seen that the power producing the phenomena was not merely a blind force, but was associated with or governed by intelligence. . . . . . The intelligence governing the phenomena is sometimes manifestly below that of the medium. It is frequently in direct opposition to the wishes of the medium. When a determination has been expressed to do something which might not be considered quite right, I have known urgent messages given to induce a reconsideration. The intelligence is sometimes of such a character as to lead to the belief that it does not emanate from any person present.

To this I may add, that in a number of recorded

cases—*e.g.*, in that of Miss Laura Edmunds, the daughter of Judge Edmunds of New York—and in several that have come under my own notice, the Intelligence is not only distinct from that of the Psychic, but uses a language unknown to the Psychic, and conveys elaborate information, precise in detail, of which he or she had no previous knowledge; and not only that, but of which no person present had any previous knowledge.

PSYCHOGRAPHY IN THE PAST.

GULDENSTUBBÉ—CROOKES.

This subject of Psychography, or writing without the intervention of ordinary human agency, is by no means new, though it has of late attracted greater attention. It has been familiar to all investigators of Psychic Phenomena, and has been called variously Direct or Independent Writing. Records of its occurrence are found in the most ancient works on the subject, and it was perfectly familiar to those early and mediæval students of occult phenomena whose researches throw so much light on that which we now find so perplexing. The most remarkable record, however, of these special facts is made by Baron Guldenstubbé, in a book entitled "*La Realité des Esprits, et le phenomene merveilleux de leur écriture directe.*"

The Baron must have been a Psychic of great power, for all the writings were obtained without the aid of any other person, and under conditions which, in most cases, would preclude the hope of successful results. It is with experiments of this nature as with all others: certain conditions are required for success. These have been, and are, much exaggerated and misrepresented, darkness being popularly supposed to be the principal desideratum. This is not so. I believe that every phenomenon — except such as require darkness for their observation, as, for instance, luminous phosphorescent appearances—can be produced in full light. Much more time and patience would be required; but, granted these, light is no final barrier to success. It is much to be regretted that more persistent attempts have not been made to produce these phenomena in such light as suffices for exact observation. The fact that this is now being done, and with such success as I shall presently show, removes one impediment to observation in the future.

Baron Guldenstubbé seems to have been able to dispense with the usual conditions under which writing is obtained—a closed room with magnetically-charged atmosphere, subdued light, and a formal gathering of persons from or through whom the necessary force is evolved. He obtained his writings anywhere, and at any time, in the open air, and on a tombstone, of which locality he was specially fond. It squared with his idea of the source of the writing, and so facilitated its execution. This, I may say in passing, is far more requisite than any other condition for success, that the Psychic through whom the force is evolved should be at ease and comfort. If he have any special ideas as to the source of the phenomenon, to controvert them by argument is to cause almost certain failure. Left to himself, with surroundings that conduce to comfort of mind and body, and with liberty to follow out his opinions as to the best means of securing results, success will usually follow.

Hence it is that the best, most sure, and most reliable phenomena are seen in private circles, where none but friends, of one mind, and united by the bonds of friendship or affection, are assembled.

Among the places named as those where successful experiments were made are the Louvre, the Museum at Versailles, the Cathedral of Saint Denis, Westminster Abbey, the British Museum, the Cemeteries of Montparnasse, Montmartre, and Père la Chaise; the Bois de Boulogne, and various churches and ancient ruins in France, Germany, Austria, and England.

The list of witnesses, twenty-seven in number, selected out of a vast number of distinguished persons who have repeatedly assisted at the Baron's experiments, includes the names of *M. Delamarre*, editor of the *Patrie; M. Choisselat*, editor of the *Univers; Mr. Dale Owen; M. Lacordaire*, brother of the great orator; *M. de Bonjochose*, the historian; *M. Kiorböe*, a well-known Swedish painter; the *Baron von Rosenberg*, German ambassador at the Court of Wurtemberg; *Prince Leonide Galitzin*, and two other representatives of the nobility of Moscow; and the *Rev. William Mountford*, who has lately contributed his personal testimony in the *Spiritualist* of Dec. 21st, 1877.

Mr. Coleman, of Upper Norwood, whose experience dates so far back, informs me that he well remembers Mr. Dale Owen going to Paris for the purpose of witnessing these remarkable experiments. He told

Mr. Coleman in detail of his accompanying the Baron and his sister Julia to various chapels in Paris, where he laid down sheets of his own paper, without pencil or writing materials; retiring a few paces, but never losing sight of the paper, he found an intelligent message written upon it in every case. Mr. Coleman has one of these curious Psychographs in his own possession. It was obtained at the Palace of the Trianon, Versailles.

The book is illustrated by thirty fac-similes of Psychographs thus obtained, and selected from more than two thousand specimens in twenty different languages, and some of them covering several pages. These were obtained between the years 1856 and 1872. The first experiment was made by placing paper and pencil in a box, which was locked, and the key of which never left the Baron's possession. No one was acquainted with the fact that any such experiment was in process. After twelve days, during which no mark was made on the paper, there appeared on it certain mysterious characters, and during that day ten separate experiments gave successful results. The box was then left open and watched, and writing was seen to grow upon the paper without the use of the pencil. From that time he abandoned the use of the pencil altogether, and obtained his vast number of Psychographs by the simple process of putting blank paper on the table of his room, or in public buildings, or on the pedestal of ancient statues, or on tombstones in churches and cemeteries. It apparently mattered little where the paper was placed; and it is more than probable that the Baron, by exercise of his will, could have obtained any given name in any given place. The association of name and statue or tomb was a consequence of his mental preposessions.

The curious reader will find a full account of these experiments made by the Baron in his book abovenamed; and for further information as to these and kindred phenomena he may consult the works, a list of which is prefixed to this volume.

Mr. Crookes, in his paper in the *Quarterly Journal of Science* above referred to, which is reprinted in his *Researches*, records two notable instances of Psychography, which I quote as showing the facility for observation in the one case, and the satisfactory result obtained in darkness, where no room existed for doubting the evidence so obtained. It is usually supposed by those who have not tried the experiment that no evidence obtained in a dark room is of any value. Mr. Crookes' record may dispel that error:—

The first instance which I shall give took place, it is true, at a dark *séance*, but the result was not less satisfactory on that account. I was sitting next to the medium, Miss Fox, the only other persons present being my wife and a lady relative, and I was holding the medium's two hands in one of mine, whilst her feet were resting on my feet. Paper was on the table before us, and my disengaged hand was holding a pencil.

A luminous hand came down from the upper part of the room, and after hovering near me for a few seconds, took the pencil from my hand, rapidly wrote on a sheet of paper, threw the pencil down, and then rose up over our heads, gradually fading into darkness.

My second instance may be considered the record of a failure. "A good failure often teaches more than the most successful experiment." It took place in the light, in my own room, with only a few private friends and Mr. Home present. Several circumstances, to which I need not further allude, had shown that the power that evening was strong. I therefore expressed a wish to witness the actual production of a written message, such as I had heard described a short time before by a friend. Immediately an alphabetic communication was made as follows—"We will try." A pencil and some sheets of paper had been lying on the centre of the table; presently the pencil rose up on its point, and after advancing by hesitating jerks to the paper, fell down. It then rose, and again fell. A third time it tried, but with no better result. After three unsuccessful attempts, a small wooden lath, which was lying near upon the table, slid towards the pencil, and rose a few inches from the table; the pencil rose again, and propping itself against the lath, the two together made an effort to mark the paper. It fell, and then a joint effort was again made. After a third trial the lath gave it up and moved back to its place, the pencil lay as it fell across the paper, and an alphabetic message told us—"We have tried to do as you asked, but our power is exhausted."

PERSONAL EXPERIENCES.

For the past five years I have been familiar with the phenomenon of Psychography, and have observed in a vast number of cases, both with recognized Psychics known to the public, and with ladies and gentlemen in private, who possess the power and readily procure the result. In the course of these observations I have seen psychographs obtained in closed and locked boxes, in a manner similar to the experiment above recorded in the case of the Baron Guldenstubbé; on paper previously marked and placed in a special position, from which it was not moved; on paper marked and put under the table, so as to get the assistance of darkness; on paper on which my elbow rested, and on paper covered by my hand; on paper inclosed in a sealed envelope; and on slates securely tied together.

I have known such writing to be almost instantaneously produced; and late experiments, to which I shall refer in their place, confirm me in the statement that the process employed is not always the same. Whereas at times the pencil is seen to write as if moved by a hand, at times invisible, but at others visibly guiding and controlling its movements, at others the writing would seem to be produced by an instantaneous effort without the use of the pencil. I recal an instance which bears on this question of the use of the pencil.

I was present at a séance held at the house of an intimate friend, three friends only present. Paper, previously initialled by each of us, was put on the floor under the table, together with an ordinary black-lead pencil. One of us, feeling the pencil against his boot, put his foot upon it, and held it there till the séance was over. Writing, however, was found on the paper; and we debated the question how it could have been done, seeing that no pencil was available for use. The paper bore our marks, and had not been removed, so far as we could tell. We met again during the same week, and I privately provided myself with the means of testing the matter. I brought a bright green pencil, and substituted it without remark for the blacklead, keeping my foot upon it all the time. When the paper was examined the writing—a very short scrawl—was found to be in green. The pencil, therefore, was used in some way unknown to me. I believe that this is the case frequently, and that instantaneous writing is done by some method other than that of the normal use of the pencil. This is noted by Baron Guldenstubbé, as I have remarked above, and was observable in some cases of slate-writing with Slade, as I shall have occasion to note hereafter; and one case at least is within my knowledge where a side of a slate is frequently covered with writing in a few seconds. The psychic in this case is a lady, whose name I have no authority to make public.

PERSONAL TESTIMONY.

I PROCEED now to give my own personal testimony as to what I have witnessed in the presence of two Psychics well known to the public, Henry Slade and Francis W. Monck, selecting those points only which bear on this subject.

I sat alone with Slade in the month of July, 1877; and I carried with me a small slate of white porcelain, taken from my own writing-desk. I held it myself under the table, at a corner furthest from Slade, and obtained a short scrawl upon it, written with a point of lead pencil which I placed upon it. Slade used ordinary slates and slate-pencil; and on one of his slates, while we held it jointly, a number of messages were written. The longest and most elaborate of these, which covered both sides of a folding-slate, was written while the slate lay on the table before me. I put my ear down to the cover of the slate, and could distinctly hear the writing in process. The sound was the grating sound of slate-pencil deliberately and carefully moved over the slate, and lasted for a considerable time; I should say three or four minutes. I noted especially the fact that the sound came from the slate immediately beneath my ear. I also observed that by a slight change of position the writing could be stopped.

In order to make my position intelligible, I append an exact diagram of the table used by Slade, which was produced in the court at the Bow Street trial, and which may now be seen by the curious at the rooms of the British National Association of Spiritualists, 38 Great Russell Street. The table used during my experiment was an old one, of about the same size, belonging to the house. It was only when this table was split into pieces that Slade had one constructed for himself. It was made of hard wood, to resist rough usage; and of remarkable simplicity, in order to be easily examined. The subjoined diagram and explanation will enable my readers to understand what Mr. Maskelyne audaciously described at the trial at Bow Street, as if it were a trick-table.

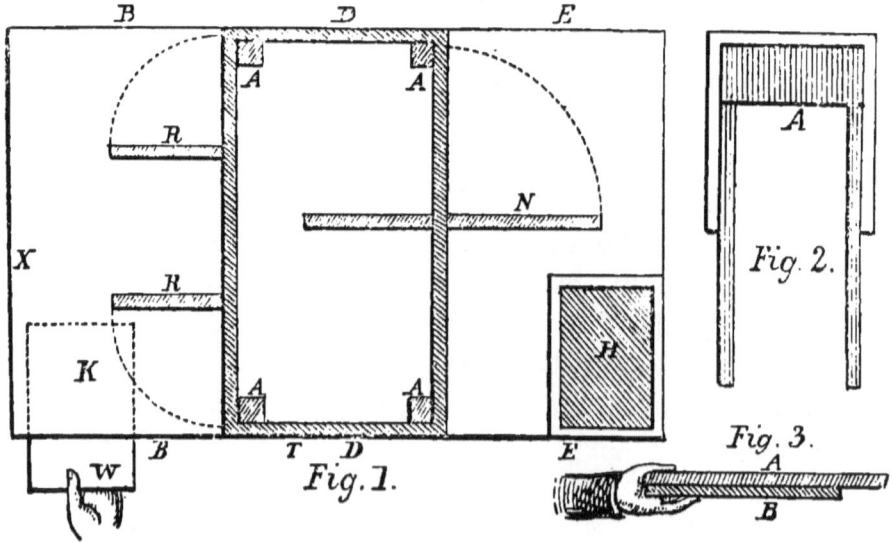

Fig. 2 represents the table Dr. Slade ordered to be brought to Bow Street; it is a kind of ordinary kitchen table, but made of ash. The frame above A was declared by the man who made it to be somewhat larger than the frames commonly used for such tables; he had made it larger, without any order to that effect, to give additional strength. There is, as usual with such tables, no frame round the flaps.

There being no veneering and no framework in each flap —nothing but an honest piece of solid ash—it is easy to see that when Dr. Slade holds a slate, B (Fig. 3), against the solid wooden flap, A, and writing comes, in dry, dusty slate-pencil, all over the upper side of the slate, in the shadow under the flap, how very disturbing such an occurrence must be to the mental equilibrium of hardened materialists.

B D E, Fig. 1, show the under side of the table, but we have put two ordinary brackets at R R, under the flap, B B, whereas Dr. Slade's table had but a single stick bracket under each flap, such as is shown at N, beneath the flap, E E. The slate "in position" is shown at H, where the stick bracket is out of its way, one of the double brackets, R, there, would have been an encumbrance, interfering with the placing of the slate. D D is the part of the table directly connected with the frame, and A A A are the tops of the four legs of the table.

Dr. Slade never sits at the flap side of the table at X. He always sits sideways, against the frame at T D, turning his feet in the direction of the lower E, and putting the slate under the table at that corner, so that the observer, who always sits at the same corner in broad daylight, has—or can have if he asks for it—Dr. Slade's hands and feet, and the edge of the slate, always in full view.

Sometimes Dr. Slade, with his thumb on the upper side of the slate at W, pushes the slate, W K, half under the table, as represented at K, then withdraws it, the whole motion being about as quick as the swing of a pendulum, yet during the moment the part of the slate K is in shadow, a sentence is scribbled across it in the dry, dusty writing of slate-pencil.

The position in which we were placed was this: Slade sat sideways at T D, and with his back to the window, through which a July sun was streaming; the blinds were up, and every corner of the room was in clear light. I sat at the side opposite to N; my right hand linked with Slade's on the top of the table, so as to form a chain, my left joining his in holding a slate at H. When my hand was raised so as not to touch Slade's hand on the top of the table, the writing at once ceased, and was resumed when contact was again made. It will be seen that other observers have noted this. Mr. F. W. Percival was especially impressed with the ease with which the writing could be stopped by breaking contact, and the rapidity with which a slight touch, even on the cuff of Slade's coat, would set it again into feeble action. He noted it in his printed testimony at the time, and has frequently mentioned it to me since.

The writing on my own porcelain slate was obtained while I held it under the corner at E, Slade not touching it.

The next piece of personal evidence which I adduce was obtained with another Psychic, F. W. Monck. The place was 26 Southampton Row; the time, Oct. 19, 1877, evening; the light, that of a small lamp, sufficient for observation; those present, the Rev. Thomas Colley, late curate of Portsmouth, Mrs. Colley, myself, and the Psychic.

I examined, carefully cleaned, and privately marked, two small school slates, which were apparently quite new; placed a tiny fragment of slate-pencil between their inner surfaces, and tied them securely together, so that they could not slip, nor could anything be inserted between them. I fastened my string, moreover, with a peculiar knot. When tied, I myself placed the slates on the table before me, and requested Mr. Colley to lay his finger on one corner, while I placed mine on the corner next to it, and Monck, who sat opposite to us, laid his hands on the corners nearest to him.

I was requested to choose some short word, and to desire to have it written within the slates. I chose *snow*. The sound of writing was distintly heard, and I was informed through Monck, entranced, that the word had been written. Three facts were then stated, viz., that a badly-formed S had been erased, and that two other letters had certain specified peculiarities in their formation.

These statements, made, be it observed, while the slates lay before me under my finger, I at once verified by untying the string that bound them together. As they had never left my sight, it is to no purpose to say that my knot was intact. Within the slates I found the word *snow* written, and with the peculiar formations and erasure which had been specified. In addition, the words "favourite way" were written. While the experiment was in process, we had been conversing about the peculiar way in which names were frequently spelt in these writings, and one of us remarked that, though a particular Christian name was frequently written, it was never spelt in the owner's *favourite way*. The passing words had been caught up and written at the moment within the slates.

Reserving comment, I note the following points in this experiment:—

1. The slates were new, clean, privately marked, and thoroughly tied.
2. They never left my sight, nor was my hand removed from them even for a moment.
3. They never were out of my own possession after I cleaned and marked them.
4. The light was sufficient for exact observation.
5. The words written could not have been prepared beforehand.
6. I have the corroboration of two witnesses.

One more case I record as a piece of personal experience, before proceeding to the experiments of others. When this subject first came before me, I endeavoured to submit it to a crucial test. For this purpose I made an experiment similar to that first made by Baron Guldenstubbé, of whose name even I had not then heard. I inclosed a piece of paper in a travelling desk of my own, which desk I strapped up in its cover, and placed in my private drawer. The key of that drawer, in which my most private papers are kept, never goes out of my possession, and assuredly I kept it consciously in view during the experiment. I left the paper undisturbed for twenty-four hours, and at the end of that time I found upon it very clear and distinct writing, covering its entire upper surface.

In this case I note the absence of any possibility of deception, conceivable to myself. At the same time, I note also the absence of corroborative testimony.

GENERAL CORROBORATIVE EVIDENCE.

STARTING, then, from the nucleus of my own experience, recorded, I pledge myself, with the most entire accuracy, so far as I am aware; I now proceed to adduce the evidence of others who have observed facts which corroborate those now recorded.

For the sake of orderly arrangement, I shall bring forward the evidence under various heads.

I.—EVIDENCE ATTESTED BY THE SENSES.

1. By the Sense of Sight.

I have already said that the evidence on which I rely most is that obtained in light which is sufficient for exact observation. I am by no means prepared to say that very satisfactory evidence may not be obtained independently of eyesight, but I am quite aware that "seeing is believing." I commence, therefore, with a record furnished by Mr. E. T. Bennett, of Manor-Villas, Richmond, and printed in *The Spiritualist* of Sept. 21, 1877.

I may premise before I go further that the language used in the records quoted is that which all Spiritualists employ. I use it without connecting myself or desiring to pledge my readers to any theory. The terms used throughout are used in their accepted signification without dispute or question.

On Sunday evening, the 9th inst., a circle consisting of Dr. Monck, Mrs F., Miss R., a medical man, Mr. Christian Reimers, and myself, met at Mr. Reimers' house, No. 6, Manor-Villas, Richmond. We sat round an ordinary table, on which were placed the works of a small musical box, two small slates, paper, and black-lead pencil. A shaded candle was placed in an adjoining room, the door being open, so that there was all through the *séance* sufficient light to see the various objects in the room, and the time by a watch.

After some ordinary preliminary manifestations, Dr. Monck's control addressed the medical man, whom I will call Dr. A., and asked him to tell him a word he would like written on the slate. The slates were examined and marked by myself, tied together securely by Dr. A. As no bit of slate-pencil could be found, a minute fragment of black-lead was placed between them, which we ascertained would make a mark. Dr. A. then chose the word "darling," and the slates were placed on the table, and Dr. M.'s and Dr. A.'s hands on them.

Dr. M.'s control: "Hav'n't you got any slate-pencil?"

Dr. A.: "No. There is a bit of black-lead in; can't you write with that?"

Dr. M.'s control: "Don't like it. Shall *we* get a bit of our own?"

Dr. A.: "Yes."

Dr. M.'s control: "My medium will carry the slates round and place them on the Doctor's head. There; it is done!"

Candle brought. The slates (which had never been out of sight of the whole circle) untied. Inside was the word "darling," written in a large, rather trembling hand, as if with *slate*-pencil, but there was none visible.

Dr. M.'s control: "Tell me the Christian name of some friend you would like to be here."

Dr. A.: "Sophia."

Dr. M.'s control: "She *is* here; and there is an old man with her, of dignified appearance. He is sorry for you about something; I think it is about money. He has such a curious thing on his head, a crown with points upwards, and little balls on them."

Dr. A.: "Will he give his name?"

Dr. M.'s control: "He says he will try and write it himself."

The medium asks for a piece of note paper, holds it in his hand a minute, places it on the table, and a pocket pencil about three inches long by it. The pencil moves, no one touching it. It makes feeble attempts to rise. Finally it succeeds, and we see it stand up by itself, and write as with a firm hand for a few seconds, and then fall down again. Dr. A. takes up the paper, and finds written the name * * * * * * *, that of a deceased nobleman with whom he had been professionally connected, and who was a relative of the lady whose name he had given, and whose rank was correctly indicated by the "curious crown."

Mr. Bennett is familiar with these phenomena, and refers them to the action of unembodied spirits, using the phraseology common to those who share this belief. He is no enthusiast, but a calm and capable observer. Nor are his records singular. I am happy to be able to call in corroboration a sceptical witness, one who is not familiar with these phenomena, who approaches them with suspicion, and is guarded in his statements, most especially in his conclusions. His prepossessions, at any rate, are not excited in our favour. My witness is a reporter for the *Malvern News*. The Psychic in this case also is Monck; and the place where the experiment took place was a house in Malvern, "into which he had never entered till the evening" in question. The account, somewhat abridged, reads thus:

Shortly after six o'clock, several ladies and gentlemen having assembled, most of them strangers to each other, sat down to an oblong deal table, which had been covered with a thick Witney blanket, the usual cover being used as a blind to darken the windows. Every particle of natural light had been shut out, and the gas turned on full. After the party had sat for some time, Dr. Monck asked for a pencil and some writing-paper. Three of the former were placed at his disposal, and he selected ours. A piece of paper was folded up, on which the pencil was put. He then borrowed some handkerchiefs, and selected ours, which he carelessly threw over the pencil and paper. In the full glare of the gas-light the pencil rose and stood upright, Dr. Monck's hands at this time being placed on his head. He removed the handkerchief, and there stood the pencil, but no writing was on the paper. A sceptical gentleman thought the pencil was sticking into the table through the blanket. At the request of Dr. Monck he lifted it up, examined it, and put it down again. It was no sooner released than it rose up again, and wrote on the paper a sentence, in the sight of all, respecting the unfavourable conditions.

Here it will be noticed that the light was ample for observation, and that the requisite darkness for the production of the writing was obtained without any interference with the facilities for exact investigation. The report concludes with a confession on the part of the reporter of inability to explain how the results "witnessed by nine sane ladies and gentlemen" were produced. "As some of them," he adds, "are well known in Malvern, they can contradict us if we have stated what is not true."

With the same Psychic, the editor of *The Medium*, Mr. James Burns, of the Spiritual Institution, 15 Southampton Row, W.C., had a noteworthy experiment, which he thus records. The persons present were himself and his wife, and the place was his own house:—

I had on the table before me several sheets of note-paper, on which I was taking notes. Dr. Monck took up a blank sheet and tore it in halves. One of these he folded up into an eighth of its original size by doubling it three times. Thus crumpled up, he placed it under a white handkerchief which lay on the table immediately before him. An ordinary elongating pocket pencil was then put beside the paper. This pencil had a screw at the point for propelling and withdrawing the lead, the handle was of a dark colour, and it had a white bone top. The light at this part of the séance was not on full, as it had been at some other parts, but there was sufficient for me to read my pencil notes. Dr. Monck, with his right hand, placed the pencil under the handkerchief, and continued to move his fingers about over the handkerchief for a few seconds. We were all intently looking for whatever might result, when Mrs. Burns exclaimed that the pencil was writing. I saw it standing up in a sloping position, with the point towards me, but as the handkerchief interposed between my view and the point of the pencil, I could not see what it was doing. Before I had much time for reflection, I saw that the pencil, besides being sloping with its point towards me, was in a violent state of motion from side to side, as if it were held by the middle and rapidly vibrated. This movement was not quite regular; sometimes the jerks made by the pencil would be longer, sometimes shorter, and complicated by movements not all in one direction. While I was trying to comprehend what this could mean, I saw it stand still, and then move gently from side to side. Mrs. Burns and Dr. Monck said, "It is crossing a word," and again the rapid vibration went on as before. In a few seconds more the pencil fell, and the handkerchief was removed, and the paper was found opened out and covered with pencil-writing in a vigorous hand.

Dr. Monck now took out his folding-slate, and gave it to me to clean. I did so carefully. He took a small crumb of slate-pencil and inclosed it between the leaves of the slate.

Dr. Monck's hand was then moved towards me, till it rested on my arm. Then it ascended to my shoulder, and lastly on to my head, where I heard and felt the tremor of writing going on in the folded slate. Shortly it was finished, and when opened a message was found written, occupying both sides of the slate.

The writing on paper took three minutes to transcribe, but it was written in about one-third of that time. The paper bore the distinctive mark of the packet from which the sheet had been taken, and one of the observers was able to watch the whole process of writing.

The slate-writing is notable on account of the evidence from two senses which attested its production.

This seems to be the place to quote a case of writing executed by a luminous hand, which was visible to at least four persons. I complicate my evidence somewhat by the introduction of a new species of Psychic phenomena, that of luminous appearances, and of hands not those of any person present. Such facts, however, are familiar to those who have witnessed these phenomena, and are attested by exact and precise observations.

The account (*Spiritualist*, Oct. 13, 1876) is written by Mr. H. D. Jencken, barrister-at-law, and the psychic was his wife, the Kate Fox of the early history of this subject. The house where the experiment was made was that of Mr. S. C. Hall, editor of the *Art Journal*. The date was Sept. 6, 1876. Nine persons were present, including Mr. and Mrs. Hall, Mr. and Mrs. Mayo, and Dr. Netherclift, of the Chelsea Infirmary.

Several efforts by the unseen beings had been made to give us "direct writing." Finally, we were ordered to hold each other's hands, and to contract the circle by drawing close up to the table. A luminous, small, beautifully-shaped hand then descended from the side at which I was sitting, that is to say, at the opposite side to Mrs. Jencken. The hand seized a pencil which was lying on the table and wrote the letters " E. W. E."

The power of holding the pencil then evidently failed. The pencil, which had been held between the forefinger and third finger, dropped on the table, and the hand raised itself high overhead, and disappeared. After a short pause it reappeared, descended, touched the table, took hold of the pencil, and wrote the words "God bless y—." At the letter *y* the strength again appeared to give way, the pencil dropped, the hand rose quickly, and was gone.

I have witnessed so many instances of direct spirit writing, that this additional instance would have been but of little attraction to me, but for the fact that others also witnessed the manifestations, some of whom were not Spiritualists, but merely witnesses. This gave interest to this séance. The hand, as sketched by me, was distinctly seen by Dr. Netherclift, Mrs. Mayo, Mr. Mayo, and others present; each of those present saw the hand from a different point of view; in other words, the objectivity of the hand was distinctly observed.

I inclose the original document, containing the direct writing, and on the right hand top of the page is the sketch of the hand. As I was drawing this sketch, several of the guests clustered round my chair, and aided me by suggesting how they each of them witnessed the writing. The luminosity around the wrist was singularly beautiful. The circumstances under which this direct writing happened were exceptionally favourable, as a test of the reality of what occurred. The sitting took place at the residence of Mr. Hall; those who were present retained the greatest self-composure. The medium was seated facing the direction whence the hand descended; the writing was done in the centre of the table, around which we were seated; the position of the hand was at right angles to Mrs. Jencken. I name these circumstances to meet in advance any theory of optical delusion, hallucination, or any other hypothesis to explain what happened.

These instances might be greatly multiplied. I do not propose to adduce more evidence of this kind, however, having other which advances my argument a step further. I have shown that the evidence of one sense attests the reality of Psychography. I now proceed to bring forward cases where the writing is heard as the pencil grates upon the slate.

2. By the Sense of Hearing.

In almost all cases where writing is produced by use of the pencil, I believe the process may be heard, especially when a slate is used. The evidence of a majority of observers makes mention of the grating noise which accompanied the writing. In several cases great pressure is used, and the pencil is appreciably worn away, remaining, too, not unfrequently, at the end of the last letter of the dusty, dry writing, that shows plainly enough how it has been employed. From a great number of cases I select the following, giving precedence to those which record experiments with Slade, and among them to the detailed narrative of the President of the Psychological Society of Great Britain:—

Having undertaken to examine without prejudice or prepossession, and to report faithfully, without favour, in a purely judicial spirit, any alleged psychological phenomena that might be submitted to me as President of the Psychological Society of Great Britain, I narrate without comment what I witnessed at a sitting with Dr. Slade this afternoon.

I sat alone with him, at three o'clock, in a room at 8 Upper Bedford Place, Russell Square, into which the sun shone brightly, at a table about five feet by four, having four legs, no ledge below, and no cloth upon it. Dr. Slade sat at one side of this table, sideways, so that his legs and feet were not under the table, but his whole body fully in my view as he faced me. I sat at the side, the corner of the table being between us. As I sat I could see half-way below the table, and by moving my head slightly, I could see the whole space below, which was wholly exposed in full daylight. An ordinary drawing-room chair was about six inches from the table on the opposite side, six feet from Dr. Slade. A heavy arm-chair was in the corner of the room, about the same distance from him and from the table. A slate of the ordinary school size and a piece of slate pencil were upon the table.

Instantly upon taking our seats very loud rapping came upon the floor. This was followed by a succession of furious blows upon the table, jarring my hands as they were laying upon it. These blows were repeated at any part of the table desired, by merely touching that spot with the finger, while the blows, as forcible as if given with a sledge hammer, were being made. Dr. Slade's hands were on the table upon my hands, and his whole body to his feet was fully before my eyes. I am certain that not a muscle moved. Then he took the slate after I had carefully inspected it, to be assured that no writing was upon it, and placing there a piece of slate pencil, the size of a small grain of wheat, he pressed the slate tightly below but against the slab of the table. Presently I heard the sound as of writing on a slate. The slate was removed, and on it a zigzag line was drawn from end to end.

* * * * * *

Blows of a more gentle kind upon the table, attended with a remarkable quivering of it, announced, as he said, that his wife was present, and desired the slate. After the slate had been carefully cleaned, it was laid upon the top of the table, with a like piece of pencil under it. Upon the slate he placed his right hand, and I placed my left hand, and with my other hand I held his left hand as it lay upon the table. As my hand lay upon the slate, I could feel, and I did also distinctly hear, something writing upon it. The communication was evidently a long one; but before I report the result, I desire to note here a remarkable phenomenon, to my mind the most suggestive that attended this experiment.

It is necessary clearly to understand the position of the parties, therefore I repeat it.

Dr. Slade and myself sat face to face. One hand of each of us was laid upon the slate. The side of the slate that was being written upon was pressed by us against the table. Our second hands were linked together, and lay upon the table. While this position was preserved, the writing proceeded without pause. When Dr. Slade removed his hand from mine it ceased instantly, and as instantly was renewed when his hand and mine met. This experiment was repeated several times, and never failed.

Here, then, was a chain or circle formed by my arms and body, and Dr. Slade's arms and body, the slate being between us, my hand at one end of it, his hand at the other end, and between our hands, and upon the slate that connected them, the writing was. When the chain was broken forthwith the writing ceased. When the chain was reformed the writing was at once resumed. The effect was instantaneous. In this curious fact we must seek the clue to this psychological mystery.

Some rapid rappings, indicating that the writing was finished, the slate was lifted, and in a clear and perfectly distinct writing the following was read. It filled the whole side of the slate:—

DEAR SERJ.,—You are now investigating a subject that is worthy of all the time you or any other man of mind can devote to its investigation. When man can believe in this truth, it will in most cases make him a better man. This is our object in coming to earth, to make man and woman better, wiser, and purer.—I am truly, A. W. SLADE.

Again the slate was cleaned and laid upon the table as before, my hand upon it. In a few seconds the following sentence was written. Considerable power was used in this writing, and I could distinctly feel the pressure of the pencil as every word was written:—

I am Dr. John Forbes. I was the Queen's physician. God bless you. J. FORBES.

Again the slate was cleaned and held under the table tight against the wood, one half of it projecting beyond the edge, so that I might be assured that it was tightly pressed against the wood; but the slate was seized, and with great force drawn away and rapidly raised above me and placed upon my head. In this position the sound of writing upon it was distinctly heard by me. On removing it, I found written upon it the following words:—

Man must not doubt any more, when we can come in this way.
J. F., M.D.

Then the large arm-chair rushed forward from the corner of the room in which it had been placed, to the table.

Again the slate was placed under the table, and projecting from it. A hand twice seized and shook my leg, both of the hands of Dr. Slade being at the moment before me, and his whole person visible.

Thus ended this experiment. All that I have reported was *done*, that is certain. How it was done, and by what agency, is a problem for psychology to solve. For my own part I can only say that I was in the full possession of my senses; that I was wide awake; that it was in broad daylight; that Dr. Slade was under my observation the whole time, and could not have moved hand or foot without being detected by me.

That it was not a self-delusion is shown by this, that any person who chooses to go may see almost the same phenomena. I offer no opinion upon their causes, for I have formed none. If they be genuine, it is impossible to exaggerate their interest and importance. If they be an imposture, it is equally important that the trick should be exposed in the only way in which trickery can be explained, by doing the same thing, and showing how it is done.

August 8th, 1876.

Mr. George King, of 11 St. George's Terrace, Gloucester Road, S.W., notes in his narrative, which I append, the fact which I have just mentioned—viz., that in his experience the crumb of pencil invariably remains at the end of the writing. This affords a strong presumption that the pencil is really used:—

At five o'clock in the afternoon of Saturday, 18th Nov. last, I repaired, by appointment, to the house of Dr. Slade. I had determined to take with me a slate of my own, and on the way I tried in four or five shops to find one to my mind. At last I secured what satisfied me—a folding slate with a varnished wooden case of somewhat peculiar construction. Each of the two flaps was seven and three-quarters inches long, by five inches wide, and had a three-quarter inch frame all round, which projected one-tenth inch above the surface. When the slate was folded there was, therefore, between the leaves a completely inclosed cavity about one-fifth inch deep, and nearly air-tight. The slate was done up in a paper parcel by the shopman, and tied with twine.

Thus armed, I presented myself at Dr. Slade's door, and was ushered into the drawing-room, where were Dr. Slade, Mr. Simmons, and two ladies. Dr. Slade and Mr. Simmons were sitting by the fire, and they invited me to take a chair beside them. Dr. Slade shortly said it was time to "light up," and he retired to a small adjoining parlour. In less than two minutes he returned and asked me to follow him. The parlour was brilliantly lighted by a gaselier suspended over a small, rickety, mahogany table in the centre of the room, and the gas remained at full power during the whole of our sitting. I examined the table, turning it over for the purpose. It had four legs attached to a frame, and was about three-and-a-half feet by two feet wide, exclusive of a flap on each side. The flap and its appurtenances on the side opposite to that at which I sat was much shattered, as if by violent usage, but on my side there did not appear to be any breakage. The flap against which I sat must originally have been intended to rest on two brackets, but one of these had been removed, so that under the corner of the raised flap which was between me and Dr. Slade there was no impediment whatever. We sat down, I against a flap of the table, with my back to the fire-place; Dr. Slade at the end of the table, on my left, with his face towards me, his left shoulder towards the table, and his legs projecting towards the fire-place. I produced my slate, and undid the wrapper. Dr. Slade had it for one instant open in his hand, but in my full view, as he dropped upon its clean surface a minute crumb of pencil. The slate was then firmly closed, and to my certain knowledge remained so till I opened it myself in the drawing-room half-an-hour afterwards. Dr. Slade proposed that it should be tied up, to which I, of course, assented. He got a piece of twine from the chimney-piece, and, while the slate was in my hands and his, the leaves were securely tied together, and the twine double knotted. Dr. Slade placed his left hand with both mine on the table, and for a few minutes held my slate in his right, but in my full view. I watched it intently all the time. He said there was a power which prevented him from putting it under the table even if he would. After a short time, as nothing came, Dr. Slade placed my slate on the table, under my left arm, and my left elbow rested on it almost till the close of the sitting. Dr. Slade never touched it again. He took a slate of his own, with a crumb of pencil on its surface, and passed it out of sight under the table, saying, "Our friends have done nothing for us yet. Perhaps they do not want to write on the gentleman's slate while I hold it. Will they write while the slate is under his arm and I am not touching it?" For a second of time scratching was heard on Dr. Slade's slate, and, when it was brought up, the words were on it "We will." He then joined his right hand to my left, his left still clasping my right, and instantly within my slate the sound of writing became audible, and continued for about ten minutes. At frequent intervals I put my ear close to the slate to listen, and there could be no mistake. The sound was low, but very distinct, and I specially noted that we could recognise the crossing of the "t's," the dotting of the "i's," and the insertion of the punctuation. It seemed as if a person were writing not rapidly, but steadily and deliberately, without jerk or pause. Two loud raps on the table announced the conclusion of the message. Dr. Slade then passed his own large slate, apparently perfectly clean and dry, half under the table, but so that I could see the other half and his hand holding it. My own slate meanwhile I placed beside my right elbow to be out of the way. Dr. Slade asked, "Can you do more for us to-night?" A scratching was heard, and the word "cannot" appeared on that portion of the upper side of his slate which had been beneath the table. The "c" was close to the side of the slate nearest to me, and far out of reach of Dr. Slade's hand, and the word was written not horizontally but perpendicularly towards Dr. Slade. The "t" was carefully crossed, and the fragment of the pencil lay where it had stopped, just at the end of the cross stroke of the "t."

We returned to the drawing-room, I carrying my own slate, and there I cut the string that bound it, and within I found a long message, entirely filling both sides of the slate and consisting of ninety-nine words, besides the signature "A. W. Slade." It was carefully written in a good firm hand, and the lines were straight and even. Each "t" was accurately crossed and each "i" was dotted. The crumb of pencil, too, was there, with one end worn away as if in writing.

Had only a few words been scrawled on my slate, it would have been, under the circumstances, astonishing, but the result actually obtained is simply confounding, when it is remembered that the quickest penman, with every facility for writing, cannot put down on paper, in long hand, with every word at full length, more than about twenty words per minute, and that writing on a slate, where there is more friction, occupies more time. By whomsoever it was done, this message must have taken *at least* five minutes to produce; but Dr. Slade had not the slate for that length of time in his hand—and, be it repeated, it had never left my sight—and for less than five seconds only was it open. As already explained, it was, except for one instant, firmly tied up with twine.

It is impossible to describe the jealous care with which I watched to detect deceit. I could discover none, nor the possibility of any. I had gone with my mind full of the evidence given in court by Messrs. Lankester and Donkin, but their alleged exposure was quite inapplicable to what took place in my presence.

On December 15th I had again an opportunity, in conjunction with a few friends, of testing Dr. Slade's alleged mediumship. We sat in our own room, at our own table, and used our own slates, one ordinary school slate, and one folding book-slate. As the *séance* was not so completely under my personal control as the previous one, it is not worth while describing it with so great minuteness. Suffice it to say that I sat next Dr. Slade, on his right hand, and that, as he always held the slate in that hand when he placed it under the table, I had every opportunity of closely watching him. We had a number of very short messages, sometimes on one slate, sometimes on the other. I observed a mark on the school slate, which, on those occasions when the slate was not passed entirely out of sight, enabled me to say positively that the writing was done on the *upper* side, and not on the under. One little circumstance seems to me very remarkable: I have already alluded to it above. When one of these messages appears, the crumb of pencil invariably remains at the point where it stops after writing the communication, forming a perfect continuation of the last stroke of the last letter. This fact, trifling in itself, to my mind, goes far to prove that the message has been written with that identical piece of pencil, and on the upper side of the slate. I do not see how otherwise it could be placed instantaneously in position with such mathematical accuracy.

The messages always purport to emanate from some invisible being. The major part come in the name of A. W. Slade, the deceased wife of the medium, but other so-called "spirits" are frequently represented, and it is a curious fact that with the change in the name of the penman the character of the handwriting completely changes too. It would be interesting to submit various specimens to a caligraphic expert. The matter of the communications appears to me to be of far less importance than the manner of their coming. The only one of any length received by me was that of ninety-nine words above mentioned. It is couched in somewhat high-flown language, and the subject is the advantages of an assured knowledge of immortality. It is very much such as a person of fair intelligence and education might utter on being suddenly asked to make a neat little speech to a total stranger.

GEORGE KING.

11 St. George's Terrace, Gloucester Road, S.W.,
Dec. 18, 1876.

This evidence receives additional corroboration from the further fact that in many cases the pencil is worn away, and great pressure has been evidently used. The following is a case in point:—

"On Sunday morning, Oct. 22nd [1876], at one o'clock, Mr. W. Metherell and Mr. G. De Carteret, of Jersey, had a *séance* with Dr. Slade, at 8 Upper Bedford Place, London, W.C. Dr. Slade produced two new slates, which were perfectly dry, and appeared never to have been used before. They were closely examined by the inquirers. Mr. Metherell then placed them together, with a crumb of pencil between, and Dr. Slade tied them firmly to each other, while Mr. Metherell held them. The tied slates were then laid on the top of the table, and Dr. Slade touched the frame of the uppermost one with one hand, whilst his other hand was held by those present. The slates never passed out of sight of the observers. A noise like that of writing was then heard, and it appeared to be executed at the ordinary speed. Dr. Slade then requested the two observers to take the slates into the next room, and to open them in the presence of two gentlemen who chanced to be there—namely, Mr. Charles Blackburn, of Didsbury, near Manchester, and Mr. W. H. Harrison, of *The Spiritualist.* The strings were accordingly cut in their presence, and the inner sides of the slates were found to be filled completely from top to bottom, and from edge to edge—with writing, including about seventy words altogether. The writing had manifestly been produced with a piece of slate pencil applied to the surface of the slate with considerable pressure."

In attestation of the truth of the foregoing statement, we append our signatures.

WM. METHERELL.   CHARLES BLACKBURN.
GEO. DE CARTERET.   W. H. HARRISON.

Mr. Wedgwood, J.P. for Middlesex, who has had a large experience in the observation of these phenomena, relates how he obtained writing in Greek and English on two new slates, which he had securely tied together. The sense of hearing detected a difference in the sound of the writing from that usually made, and when the slates were untied, this was satisfactorily accounted for by the presence of the Greek characters. The material part of Mr. Wedgwood's evidence is as follows:—

I breathed on the slates, and rubbed them well with my pocket-handkerchief, and putting the rubbed faces together, we tied them up fast with a piece of cord, with a fragment of slate-pencil between them. Thus tied up, the slate was laid flat on the table, without having been taken under it at all or removed for a moment from under my eyes. I placed both my hands upon it, and Slade one of his. Presently we heard the writing begin, coming distinctly from the slate as I leaned down my ear to listen to it. It did not sound, however, like running writing, as we both remarked, but like a succession of separate strokes, as if someone was trying to write and could not make his pencil mark, and I expected that it would prove an abortive attempt. It went on, however, with the same kind of sound for a long time, perhaps for six or seven minutes. At last there was a decided change in the sound, which became unmistakably that of rapid writing in a running hand. When this was done, I took the slates into the other room, leaving Slade entranced behind, and untying them, I found that on one face was written in a very good hand the 26th verse of the 1st chapter of Genesis, in Greek, from the Septuagint, and on the other a message of the usual character in English running hand. The Greek letters, being each written separately, was what had given the broken sound of the former part of the writing, the change from which to the continued sound of running writing had been so striking.

If it be suggested that the slates were really prepared beforehand with some invisible writing which was brought out by the heat of my hand, I answer (independent of other grave objections) that the writing as it stands can be wiped out by the merest touch, and could not possibly in its supposed invisible state have escaped obliteration when the slates were well rubbed by my pocket-handkerchief.

H. WEDGWOOD.

The same result is noted by observers who have carried with them their own slates, and have taken special precautions to prevent deception. A lady whose name I have no authority to publish, but who is known to me, and who professes her readiness to give private testimony if desired, records a very interesting experiment with Slade (Aug. 16, 1876), in which she and a friend succeeded in getting writing on her own slate while it lay upon the table in broad light, with her friend's elbow resting upon it. In every case—the experiment was repeated several times—the writer "could distinctly hear sounds of writing on the slate." The record further proceeds, noting that cessation of writing when the chain was broken by removing the hands, of which I have already spoken:—

> Dr. Slade then moved across the room to procure a larger slate; this we examined to satisfy ourselves that there was nothing written upon it. The slate was then placed under the table, with a small piece of slate-pencil upon it, Dr. Slade holding it with his right hand, and my friend with his left. My friend said he kept the slate as close as possible to the table, but the pressure caused by the writing seemed to force it downwards. The result of this was, that shortly, a distinct sound of rapid writing was heard upon the slate, and a message, of which the following is a copy, was found to have been written:—
>
> Dear Friends,—It is an undeniable fact that man is more willing to receive the mysterious than he is to receive plain teaching that appeals to his own reason, and will be approved by it. Now all theologians of the present day have the Bible for their foundation; they *all* differ. Now as they express the Bible it is the most mysterious book man's eyes ever beheld; everything there set down is clothed in mystery, when you look at it from *this standpoint*. Christ told the multitudes that he came to establish a new law, that he came to fulfil a mighty mission, but how few that follow his teaching, or follow his laws of love. Spiritualism comes and brings its own proof, as this letter is proof of the presence of A. W. SLADE.

This message covered the whole side of the slate which had been *next* to the table. The lines were close together, and extremely evenly kept. We were conversing with Dr. Slade more or less all the time the writing continued, and I noticed that whenever I loosed his hand the writing ceased; when I again held it it continued.

I was anxious to have a few words written upon my slate while I alone held it, which I might presume to show to my friends. Dr. Slade requested me to move near him, so I changed places with my friend, and held the slate with my left hand close under the table. The medium first made a few passes down my left arm with his right hand, then placed it so that all our five hands met in the centre of the table; the only one which was invisible being my left, which was holding the slate. In this position, and while my foot was upon the medium's left foot, his other to be plainly seen, I heard and felt the pencil writing, and on looking found upon my slate, which had been held by my own hand alone, " Good-bye; God bless you. ALLIE."

The same results, I may here add, are obtained by Slade at the present time. *La Renovation*, a paper published in Belgium, has lately contained a long article detailing the experiences of Canon X. Mouls with Slade. The usual examination of the table, and preparation of slate and fragment of pencil, having taken place, Slade held the slate under the table. " Suddenly," says the Canon, " we heard a kind of grating noise, and presently a knock, which signified that the slate could be withdrawn. Upon it were two sentences, one in French, the other in English." On another occasion, the Canon took his own slate, held it himself, and again distinctly heard writing going on. What was written was found to be a long extract from the New Testament, beautiful in caligraphy, and with the straight lines exactly preserved.

The Baroness von Vay, a name well known to English investigators of these subjects, lately writes to a friend after having seen Slade at the Hague, whither he went after his departure from England:—

Our séance with Mr. Slade, at the Hague, was one of the best ones. I am fully convinced, and so is the Baron, of that medium's genuineness and good character.

We sat in full daylight at midday, and got spirit-writing upon our *own* slates, Slade holding them upon the Baron's head. He (my husband) felt the writing upon the top of his head, and we heard it distinctly. Then Slade held the slate upon the Baron's shoulder, and again a message was written.

Not to multiply instances respecting the phenomena observed with this special Psychic, I pass to records which show that the sense of hearing bears similar testimony to the reality of the phenomena observed with Francis W. Monck.

Mr. George H. Adshead, of Derby, who has had great opportunity of experiment with this Psychic, records (Sept. 17 and 18, 1876) a remarkable case of the nature now under notice. The meeting was held at 27, Uttoxeter Road, Derby; the light was good, clear gas-light. Present, Mrs. Ford, Mr. Oxley, of Manchester; Mr. W. P. Adshead, of Belper; and Mr. and Mrs. G. H. Adshead, of Derby.

Omitting all notice of other phenomena, I notice two cases of Psychography which occurred, one on each evening. Mr. Adshead brought and placed a box on the table. A piece of paper was initialled by those present, and placed, together with a lead pencil, in the box, which was then securely tied up with tapes, and these were knotted at the crossings and sealed. On opening the box there were found on the paper several sentences which had been dictated by the company.

After this Mr. W. P. Adshead cleaned a slate, placed some pencil upon it, and held it under the table, in close contact with the top of it. Monck held the other end. Mr. Adshead thus describes what took place:—

We asked that there might be written on the upper surface, "The former things are passed away," "Blessed are the pure in heart, for they shall see God." We heard the pencil writing, and on bringing the slate up found the above sentences written on it in a clear, neat hand. The experiment was repeated. Mr. Oxley held one end this time, and the sound of writing was heard, and a sentence suggested by one of the company was found written on the clean side of the slate. The slate did not pass from my brother's hand from the moment he held it under the table after cleaning it until he brought it up with one side covered with writing. Mr. Oxley was equally positive of the same when he held it. They each felt Dr. Monck pulling vigorously at his end of the slate, and they exerted a similar force at their end, so that it was clear the Doctor's hand was not free, and his disengaged hand was resting on the table.

Séance No. 2, September 18th.—There were eight persons present, three ladies and five gentlemen. A lady whom Dr. Monck had never before seen had a slate passed to her by a sitter, which she examined and found clean, the slate-pencil which was on the table a few minutes before we sat down could not be found. An investigator suggested that it would be a good test if a lead-pencil were used.

Accordingly a lead-pencil was put on the slate, and the lady held both under the table; the sound of writing was instantly heard, and in a few seconds a communication had been written filling one side of the slate. The writing was done in lead, and was very small and neat, and alluded to a strictly private matter. Here were three tests at once:—
1. Writing was obtained without the medium (or any other person but the lady) touching the slate from first to last.
2. It was written with a lead-pencil at the spontaneous suggestion of another stranger. 3. It gave an important test-communication regarding a matter that was strictly

private. Dr. Monck did not so much as touch the slate from first to last.

Mr. E. H. Valter, of 51 Belgrave Road, Birmingham, testifies to the same effect. The senses of both hearing and feeling testified to the fact of the production of the writing at the time of observation.

Dr. Monck asked any person present to clean a small folding-slate. This done, he placed a small fragment of slate-pencil on the slate, and closed it. He then placed it on the head of any of the persons present, and requested them to place their hands upon the slate, so as to be quite certain that it did not go out of their possession. The pencil inside the slate was then both heard by those present to be writing, and the person who had the slate upon his head could also feel the pressure caused by the pencil in writing. The time occupied in writing the communication was only a few seconds, according to its length, but considerably less time than any person could possibly have written it in. These manifestations took place in the light, so that all the movements of Dr. Monck were closely scrutinised. The following are some of the messages given. The words underlined [printed in *Italic*], and also those words with a capital, are exactly as they were written on the slate:—

"Truth is *four square*, and cannot be *displaced*.
"SAML."

"Great is the Truth, and it must prevail.
"SAML. August 21st, 1876."

"We love you, and are ever about your paths, studying your well-being, and actively co-operating with you in every good word and work.
"SAML. Tuesday evening, Aug. 22, '76."

"It is as difficult to shut out from humanity the truth of Spirit-intercourse, as to exclude the daylight from this room.
"SAML. Tuesday morning, Aug. 22, '76."

This last communication was given on the morning of the 22nd of August. We had just been observing to each other that the bright rays of sunlight were rather troublesome, so that the message was very *à propos*. Many other messages were given, some were written on note-paper, marked by all present, so as to be certain that another paper was not substituted, and under these conditions the messages were still given, in the light, and Dr. Monck's hands clearly in view.

The messages or writings are of the usual type, and I lay no stress upon their substance. I direct attention solely to the fact of their presence; and I reiterate my desire to seek a solution of the question, How is writing done under such circumstances at all? To say that the matter of the writing is silly does not dispose of the fact that writing is there. By what method is it executed?

EXPERIMENTS WITH OTHER PSYCHICS.

I HAVE hitherto alluded only to Slade and Monck as the vehicles of this force, and the Psychics in whose presence these phenomena are produced. Though they afford us, by virtue of their prominence before the public, most available evidence, it must not be supposed that abundant facts of a similar description are not to be found in other quarters. I am precluded from referring to cases where the Psychic is not before the public. For obvious reasons, ladies and gentlemen do not voluntarily expose themselves to the curiosity of those who, only too frequently, reward information given by an incredulous stare, or an insinuation of delusion or imposture. When the plain facts are so far recognised that a profession of belief in their reality does not involve social stigma, or suspicion of a latent craziness, many persons will step forward to give their own testimony. That they do not now do so is not surprising; but the fact remains, though I cannot make use of it for purposes of argument, that these phenomena occur in the privacy of domestic life, are witnessed in many a family where no stranger is admitted, and where no aid in the evolution of the phenomena is sought.

I have records of experiments with two American Psychics, which I adduce here by way of corroboration. The first is given by the Hon. J. L. O'Sullivan, formerly American Minister at the Court of Portugal, and his experiments were made with Mrs. Harman of San Francisco. The power of obtaining this phenomenon was rapidly developed in her within three weeks, and the progress made was very sudden. The noise made by the act of writing, it will be noted, was different from that observed with Slade, though the more familiar sound of cursive writing could apparently be imitated at will.

Mr. O'Sullivan thus describes what he saw:—

The *modus operandi* was this. The slate (sponged clean with a small piece of pencil laid upon it, at first like Slade's, but afterwards, by direction, considerably bigger) was held under a common table, about a couple of inches below the table-top, she holding one corner between her thumb and fingers, and I supporting it lightly between mine, at the opposite diagonal corner of the slate. Our other hands were on the top of the table. In this situation it is clear that if she had relaxed her hold, to make any other use of her fingers, the slate must have dropped instantly to the ground, so light was the support contributed to it by me. Nay, more—I having once asked to have my hand touched, there was then written on the slate that I should place my entire hand on the top of the slate, which I did, so that the slate was then held up solely by her thumb and fingers at one corner of it. My hand was then touched, stroked, and patted, and a ring on the little finger taken off, at my request, dropped audibly on the slate, and again put on, with some little difficulty in pushing it over the thickness of the joint.

Sometimes, too, she laid the slate on the open palm of her hand, and then directed me to place my hand under hers, so that the entire back of her hand rested on the palm of mine, both hands thus uniting in holding the slate up to within an inch or two of the under side of the table top. Both of these modes of holding the slate certainly constituted the most complete of test conditions as to the point that the medium's hand could not possibly have had anything to do, either with the touching mine and taking off the ring, or with the copious writing on the slate, which would take place as will be seen below. These things were certainly done by no mortal hand. She and I were alone in the room; the table was a common everyday one, standing on an unbroken spread of carpet: will Dr. Carpenter consider that they come within the reach of " unconscious cerebration"?

Another point as to the *modus operandi*, which differs from the experiences with Dr. Slade. While the slate was being held under the table, we would not hear the scratching of the pencil in the act of writing, *but a steady stream as of rapid little ticks on the slate*, for all the world like the sound of a stream of electric sparks. We would then hear three loud ticks and the sound of the pencil dropping on the slate, as a signal that it was done. We would withdraw the slate, and *there* would be the message, always distinctly written. And yet, on my once remarking on this circumstance as being different from what occurred at Dr. Slade's, and also with Mrs. Francis (another slate-writing medium at San Francisco), the next time we heard, first the flow of the stream of ticks, and then the scratching sound of writing with a slate pencil, as though to show that they could do that too if they chose.

It was also to be noted that a communication of some length would be given in broken parts, even a sentence being sometimes broken off in the middle. The signal for stopping would be given, as though for rest and recuperation of the force. This will be illustrated below. Seldom would more than twenty or twenty-five words be given consecutively without such an intermission, long enough for me to read, copy, expunge, and rub the slate, and again restore it to its position under the table. It seemed as though some force analogous to electricity flowed down the medium's arm, so as to charge the slate and pencil with some spiritual power, so as to establish the conditions under which the spirit hands were able to act. That no mortal hands were, or could possibly have been there, was, I repeat, absolutely certain.

There is now before the public in America a Psychic of very great power, Charles E. Watkins, of Cleveland, Ohio. From several accounts of phenomena observed in his presence, I select now what bears upon my present point, but I shall have reason to recur to him again before my argument is complete.

My friend, Mr. Epes Sargent, of Boston, U.S.A., who is indefatigable in his attempts to convince an unwilling world that there is in and around us something more than materialists would have us to believe, has published in the *Spiritualist* of Oct. 12, 1877, a very precise account of his experiments with Watkins. On the 18th of September, he tells us, he bought a new slate, protected by paste-board covers, and repaired to Watkins' temporary residence, 46 Beach Street, Boston. Apparently Mr. Watkins was in a very unsuitable frame of mind—worried, out of temper, ill at ease—just the worst state, one would say, for hope of success in an experiment which demands, above all, passivity and ease in the Psychic. It does not seem, however, to have made much difference in the present instance.

Mr. Sargent was alone, and the time was about noon on a clear, bright September day. The phenomena all centred round a belief in intercourse with the Spiritual world. Mr. Sargent wrote six names on six different slips of paper, concealing the movement of his hand from Watkins, who, however, had turned his back and made no effort to see what was being written. "Without touching the pellets—only pointing at them with a slate-pencil—Watkins gave the name written on each." Mr. Sargent unfolded them one by one, and found that in every instance he was right. His power of clairvoyance was very strong, and I think it likely that this supersensuous condition is a frequent concomitant of the state in which Psychography becomes possible.

Mr. Sargent's narrative, so far as it bears on my present subject, reads thus:—

He now handed me two slates, which I cleaned thoroughly with a wet towel, which I had asked for. The theory that by some chemical process there might be some writing upon a slate ineffaceable by scrubbing, but made visible after a minute or two, was wholly disproved by subsequent occurrences. Mr. Watkins did not touch the slates after I had washed them. He simply placed a crumb of slate-pencil between them, and told me to hold them out at arm's length. This I did, first satisfying myself once more that they did not bear the mark of a single letter on any of their surfaces. I held the two joined slates out in my left hand, the medium being some four feet distant from them. "Do you hear writing?" asked he. I put my ear down, and distinctly heard the light scratching of the bit of slate-pencil. "It is finished," said he, as a slight rap came on the slate. I did not see how there could have been time for more than a simple name to have been written; but when I took one slate from the other, there, on the surface of the lower slate, was a letter of *fifty-four words*, signed with the name of a deceased brother, which name I had not written down among those on the pellets. The letter was characteristic, but gave no startling proof of the writer's identity. The hand-writing had a general resemblance to my brother's, but I omitted to take steps to compare it carefully before the writing was rubbed out.

A still better test was in store for me. The little slate, in stiff pasteboard covers, which I had bought an hour before, and brought with me, had rested untouched near my right elbow on the table. Mr. Watkins now took it up, lifted a cover, put a crumb of slate-pencil on the surface of the slate, closed the cover, and handed the slate to me. I *know* that there was no manipulation, no delay, no possibility of trick on his part. I *know* that no "prepossession" or expectancy of my own was a possible factor in the case, if I can be permitted to use my reason in saying so. I looked at the slate on both sides—satisfied myself (though there was no occasion for this under the circumstances) that it had not been tampered with, then held it out, and the name written on it was *Anna Cora Mowatt*, afterwards *Ritchie*, whose funeral I attended at Kensal-Green in London, when Mr. Varley, Mr. D. D. Home, Mrs. Cox, Mr. Harrison, and other Spiritualists were present.

I held my own slate out a second time, and then came the words: "*My dear brother.— Yours, Lizzie.*" Her name had not been even written or uttered by me up to this time. *Lizzie* was the name by which we had always called her, though she usually signed herself Elizabeth.

Again I held out my own slate, and there came the words:—"*My dear son, God bless you. Your father, who loves you dearly.—Epes Sargent.*"

During these intervals the slate was held by me, and there was no possible way by which any *human* trick or jugglery could have been practised. The sunshine still streamed into the room; the medium sat there before me; no other person was present. No more stringent conditions could have been demanded, even by Messrs. Lankester and Donkin. The medium, however, writhed as if in torture every time the slate-writing took place. It was evidently accompanied by some powerful nervous excitement on his part.

Mr. Chas. E. Watkins is twenty-nine years old, and a man of a highly nervous and sensitive temperament. He is a far different person intellectually from what I had been led to expect. He showed, by flashes, a high order of mind, and I regret that I could not have taken down in shorthand some of his remarks.

He now took my slate, and, after I had re-examined it, he held it out in his own hand, and in less than ten seconds one side was fully covered with a letter from my sister Lizzie. Here it is:—

Spirit-land.

MY DEAR BROTHER,—

I come to you this morning with my heart full of love for you, and I think that perhaps you may *believe* that it is me, your own sister. George is here with me.   Your loving sister,
LIZZIE.

If you ever doubt spirit communion, look at this slate.
Your sister,
LIZZIE.

I still have the slate, with the writing uneffaced. There were no punctuation marks, but the word "believe" was underlined. The whole was written in less than twelve seconds.

His brother, Mr. James Otis Sargent, a man of calm and clear mind, and a thoroughly capable observer, also went to experiment with Watkins, and his testimony corroborates that of Epes Sargent. He is good enough to send me the following account of an interview with C. E. Watkins, at his room, No. 46 Beach Street, Boston, on the 19th day of September, 1877:—

Watkins and myself were the only persons present. He handed me some slips of paper on which I wrote the names of five deceased persons, folding up each paper as soon as I had written the name upon it, so that its contents were thoroughly concealed. While I was doing this, W. left the room.

When he came back, the five folded papers, all mixed together, lay on the table under my right hand. Without touching them, he requested me to pick out one of them and hold it in my left hand. I did so. After walking across the room once or twice, and laying his hand on my head, he told me correctly the name that was written on the paper. In like manner, he told me the names written on the remaining papers, while I held them, one by one, tightly grasped in my hand.

I now threw the papers aside, and took the slates, two of which, precisely alike, were lying on the table. I cleaned each slate carefully on both sides with a damp towel. Watkins then sat down at the table, opposite me, laid one slate on the table, bit off a little piece of slate-pencil and laid it on the slate, put the other slate over it as a cover, placed his two hands flat on that, and told me to put my hands on his, which I did. In a moment he drew out his own hands, so that my hands were left with the slates beneath them. Then he said that if I put my ear down I would hear the pencil writing. I put my ear down (not forgetting, however, to keep an eye upon him), and I heard distinctly the sound of the pencil. While I was listening, the pencil gave three slight taps, and then the sound stopped.

I lifted the upper slate, and on the under one two communications were written. The first purported to come from a deceased brother, whose name was on one of the papers; the second from my father, whose name I had not written. The handwriting of the two was quite different. I did not recognise it. But the signature of the second communication, in the peculiar form of some of the letters, was like my father's signature.

The slates were now cleansed again, the bit of pencil was placed between them, and I held them myself at arm's length, *Watkins not touching them or me.* On opening them I found a short communication signed with another of the names that I had written. The next time Watkins held the slates, and a message appeared purporting to be from a deceased sister named in one of my papers.

Here the séance ended. It took place in broad daylight. I watched every movement of the medium, and there was no possibility of fraud. There was nothing in the messages by which I could identify them as coming from the persons named; but that they were written by some mysterious agency I have no doubt.   JAMES OTIS SARGENT.

Cedar Square, Roxbury,
Nov. 20, 1877.

Mr. John Wetherbee, of Boston, U.S.A., gives a similar testimony. He is a well-known writer on Psychological subjects, and has devoted prolonged attention to them. Few writers in America are more entitled to speak on these subjects, or command more attention by their utterances. He testifies thus:—

I followed an impression I had, and bought two new slates at a store, and had holes bored in the frames, and tied the two slates together, and sealed the knots. The slates were clean, and the medium never touched or saw the inside of them. I had charge of them, and they were never out of my sight. The room was as light as a clear afternoon sun shining into it could make it. The tied slates lay on the table before me and before him—not under table, but on the table. It took some little time, for the new slates were not in so good mesmerically charged condition as the slates in his common use are; but I felt as though I would like to have the writing on the new slates, so I was patient, and was well paid for my patience, for after a while I heard the atom of pencil that I had put in the slates before tying them together beginning to write, after which I cut the strings, and found one of the slates filled with a communication signed by the name of a well-beloved friend and relative who died some seven years ago.

Now, my good reader, I know—as well as I know that the sun has shone to-day—*first*, that, as I said, the slates were new and clean; *secondly*, that no one in the room or out of the room (the only occupants being the medium and myself) wrote the communication on the slate; and, *thirdly*, that it must have been done by an invisible, intelligent being or beings, and could not have been done in any other conceivable way. I make this statement as strongly as I know how, and my oath shall be attached if needed.

I had many communications besides the one described with the tied slates. I will describe one which was on his own slates, but just as good a test, for my eyes are open and my head is level. I took *his* two slates, and washed them clean, and laid one on the other, like a double slate, and held them out at arm's length, and three feet or more from the medium, and he never once touched them; the bit of pencil began to write; I had put it between the upper and under slates; then I opened them, and on each slate was an intelligent communication—one from a relative and one from a friend. Both, it will be seen, were written at the same time, both by different spirits and on different subjects, and the handwriting of each was very different also.

Dr. H. B. Storer, 29 Indiana Place, Boston, has the same story to tell. I give his record:—

I took his own two slates, first examining them, to know, as I positively do, that there was no writing upon them. I placed them together, the medium simply dropping a crumb of slate-pencil between them, and held them at arm's length in my left hand, in the bright light of the sun, the medium sitting within about three feet of the slate, convulsively writhing, while the noise of scratching was feebly heard, apparently on the slates. In some two or three minutes, I should think, he said: "It is done," and I separated the slates and found a short message written in a large, bold hand, and signed "Dr. Warren." I know that some invisible but intelligent being, other than the medium or myself, wrote that message, and such a being I call a spirit.

Mr. Chester A. Greenleaf writes from Chicopee, Mass., under date, Nov. 14th, 1877:—

My wife received a long communication on new double slates bought and screwed together by myself, and untouched by Watkins. The moving of the tiny pencil was heard by her while Watkins was standing in a doorway about twelve feet distant from where the slates were held by her.

Mr. Watkins seems to obtain this phenomenon under

almost any prescribed condition. It is recorded of him (Aug. 25 ult.) that he submitted his powers to a crucial testing on the public platform. Two new slates were bought, and kept in the possession of the chairman of the meeting, Dr. Beals, and by him carried to the platform. A committee, consisting of two gentlemen who are not believers in the phenomena called Spiritual, and one who is, was chosen from the audience. The usual preparations having been made, the slates were held by Watkins and the three gentlemen. " Soon the scratch of the pencil was heard, and on taking the slates apart, a message of fifty words was found on one of them ; the committee affirming the impossibility of any substitution of slates, or of chemical writing."

I have now brought forward testimony sufficient for my purpose. If what I have adduced does not establish my case, then no amount of proof would suffice. I pass to another class of evidence.

II.

EVIDENCE FROM THE WRITING OF LANGUAGES UNKNOWN TO THE PSYCHIC.

It is a by no means uncommon thing for the handwriting in which the messages are written to be one totally different from that of the Psychic; and it is a noteworthy fact that when a special handwriting is associated with a special signature, that association (so far as I have seen) is always preserved. I am acquainted with many cases in which this is very observable. I have now before me a specimen of Psychography obtained in private without the intervention of any one outside the family circle, in which the writing is so minute as to be illegible without the use of a strong magnifying-glass. Yet the letters are clearly and beautifully formed, the lines are straight and regularly spaced, and the capitals and the name of the Supreme Being are written large, and with great care in their formation. The same half-sheet of notepaper which contains this specimen contains also another message, written in a totally different handwriting, but also with great neatness and care. Each is signed by a name, or rather by a designation, and each contains coherent and sensible matter. Each handwriting has been preserved exactly in all communications made now for some five years; and no variation is discernible between the writing when obtained without human intervention, as in the case above quoted, and that which is automatically written through the hand of the Psychic through whom these messages are given. There is an absolute identity preserved throughout.

It is not only that the character of the writing is the same, but there is a marked presence in these messages of individuality on the part of the Intelligence. The matter of the message is as marked as the manner of it. This is observable especially in writings obtained under the best conditions of privacy in a family circle. Those who have looked carefully into the laws which govern these phenomena do not expect to gain any information that merits attention amid the distracting surroundings of a public circle, where the Psychic is valuable chiefly for the unfavourable conditions under which he can manage to give evidence to a sceptical inquirer; where the performance is a species of psychical gymnastics, conditions being prescribed for the special purpose, apparently, of rendering it impossible to produce a given result; and success being the invariable signal for still more stringent demands. Such investigators, it is presumed, have their reward.

In private, on the contrary, when the method of production is familiar, and the attention is directed more to the nature of information given, there is observable a very distinct and marked individuality in the Intelligent operator, and much that is written is worthy of attention on its merits.

Almost invariably this individuality is not akin to that of the Psychic. When only one Intelligence can be detected, then usually the broad characteristics of the Psychic are reproduced, but with a marked variation in minute points, and with either the absence of some strong personal peculiarity, or with the addition of one equally forcibly marked. And where several Intelligences can be traced, they differ among themselves as strongly as they do from the Psychic.

Not only do these Intelligences present characteristics of form and style of communication different from what would have been used by the Psychic, but they give information which is beyond his knowledge, and sometimes use a language with which he is not acquainted. It is not my purpose now to dwell on the fact that information is given by means of these messages which neither is nor ever has been within the knowledge of the special Psychic through whom the phenomenon was caused. That would lead me into details which do not rightly belong to my subject, and I should manifestly be compelled to narrow down my argument to such cases as are within my own private knowledge. It is impossible to say of a given public Psychic, like Monck or Slade, that he does or does not know such a fact, or has or has not ever heard of it in his past life. I could only say that it was unlikely that he has such out-of-the-way knowledge, and could ground no argument on such an opinion.

It is easier to adduce evidence as to the language used. When we find Ancient and Modern Greek, Spanish, Portuguese, Russian, Swedish, Dutch, German, Arabic, and Chinese forming the language of some of these Psychographs, obtained in the presence of Slade and Watkins, we shall not have much difficulty in concluding that their linguistic attainments are not of this polyglot character. As a matter of fact, Watkins is a young man whose past life has not been one that has been favourable to the acquisition of any knowledge, except that gained in the hard school of experience; and Slade knows no language but his own mother tongue. I am in a position to affirm this with confidence, on the authority of Dr. Carter Blake, who was accustomed to read French with Miss Slade and Miss Simmons during their stay in London. He says, in a letter to me, "We used to act little plays by Molière, and the like. I am certain that Slade, who was generally present, was entirely and hopelessly ignorant of every word. . . . . Simmons is as ignorant of the 'ethnic' languages as Slade, and the girls have a very moderate school-girl acquaintance with the French language alone."

I adduce, therefore, this fact, that languages unknown to the Psychic are frequently used, as an additional proof of the absence of fraud. When such precautions are taken to prevent previous fraudulent preparations of the slates as I have noted in each quoted case, the presumption is in favour of the reality of the phenomenon. When the evidence of the senses tells of the progress of the writing, that presumption is increased. If, when the slate is inspected, the language used is one unknown to the Psychic, I submit that the presumption is still further increased, and that another link has been added to the chain of evidence.

I have already mentioned one case, that of Mr. Hensleigh Wedgwood, J.P., in which his ear detected the sound of Greek writing, and afterwards of the cursive script of English. I will add two other cases, one recorded by the Hon. R. Dale Owen, formerly American Minister at the Court of Naples. It dates back to a time when Slade was comparatively unknown in this country. The record is curious, inasmuch as Mr. Owen had the slate and papers on his knees, and saw the detached hand, like those mentioned by Mr. Crookes and Mr. Jencken, which executed the writing:

At half-past seven on Monday evening, Feb. 9th, 1874, I called at Dr. Slade's rooms, 413 Fourth Avenue, New York, found him disengaged, and had a sitting which I shall remember while I live.

It was held in his back parlour; no one but myself present; doors closed and locked; sufficient gaslight from a chandelier suspended above the table to make every object in the room distinctly visible. We sat at a table without cover, five feet by two and a half, Slade at one end, and I on one side, near him; Slade's hands on the table *throughout the sitting*.

An interval of some ten or fifteen minutes during which nothing occurred; Slade nervous, restless, and seemingly disappointed. Then he laid a small slate on the table before me, and, after a time, went to a writing-desk, brought thence half a quire of paper, selected a sheet, and handed it to me with a request that I would examine it. I did so, carefully, under the gaslight, and can positively affirm that not a word or letter was visible upon it. Thereupon he added, " They wish you to lay it on the slate, and to lay the slate on your knee."

Then, after another pause: "Have you a lead pencil?"
"Yes."
"Please throw it under the table."
I did so.

A few minutes afterwards I felt the grasp as of a hand on one of my knees, arresting my attention, for the touch was unmistakably distinct. Presently there appeared, stealing over my knees, and creeping slowly up the slate, a hand, holding my pencil. This hand resembled, point for point, that of a white marble female statue, alike in size, in colour, and in form; the fingers taper, and the whole most delicately moulded. *It was detached and shaded off at the wrist. It commenced writing about the middle of the note sheet, and continued to write under my eyes for two or three minutes*, ending at the bottom of the page. Then it slipped gently back under the table, carrying the pencil with it.

Again an interval, perhaps of five minutes. Then appeared a second hand, somewhat smaller than the first, but in colour and symmetry closely resembling it. This hand moved to the top of the sheet of paper, wrote as the former had done, and for about the same period of time, then disappeared slowly in like manner. I saw it even more distinctly than the first, because it wrote outside of the shadow of the projecting table-top, and directly under the gaslight.

As we had no raps indicating the close of the sitting, we kept our places, talking over what had happened. After some time, a hand similar to that which first wrote, showed itself coming out from below the end of the table furthest from Dr. Slade. It was detached, as the others had been, remained visible several minutes, then sank out of sight. This closed the sitting.

When I came to examine the writing of which I had thus witnessed the execution, I found the first written to be in English, a commonplace communication with the signature of Dr. Slade's deceased wife. The last written, but first on the note sheet (headed in English, "Law of Love. Matt. v. 43—45"), was in Greek.

Now, my knowledge of Greek, imperfect when I left college, has, during more than half-a-century of disuse, so faded out that I can barely translate a word, here and there. I

Law of love — Matth. 5:43-45.

Ἠκούσατε ὅτι ἐρρέθη. Ἀγαπήσεις τὸν πλησίον σου καὶ μισήσεις τὸν ἐχθρόν σου. 44 ἐγὼ δὲ λέγω ὑμῖν ἀγαπᾶτε τοὺς ἐχθροὺς ὑμῶν ευλογεῖτε τοὺς καταρωμένους ὑμᾶς καλῶς ποιεῖτε τοὺς μισοῦντας ὑμᾶς καὶ προσεύχεσθε ὑπὲρ τῶν ἐπηρεαζόντων ὑμᾶς, καὶ διωκόντων ὑμᾶς 45 ὅπως γένησθε υἱοὶ τοῦ πατρὸς ὑμῶν τοῦ ἐν οὐρανοῖς, ὅτι τὸν ἥλιον αὐτοῦ ἀνατέλλει ἐπὶ πονηροὺς καὶ ἀγαθούς, & καὶ βρέχει ἐπὶ δικαίους & καὶ ἀδίκους.

Dear Friend & Brother. R.D.O.
We are pleased to see the Eyes of Men open, and ready to receive the light that will help develope goodness in their hearts and Souls —
then peopl can see the goal of this great truth, as many ask what good can you find in Spiritualism as soon as show them the goal. If they would follow our good teachings. — A W Slade

referred the manuscript to two of the best Greek scholars in Harvard University, and from them I ascertained that it was what it purported to be (a few aspirates and accents only omitted), the original of the three well-known verses, thus rendered in our revised version :—

"43. Ye have heard that it hath been said, Thou shalt love thy neighbour and hate thine enemy.

"44. But I say unto you, love your enemies, bless them that curse you, do good to them that hate you, and pray for them which despitefully use you and persecute you.

"45. That ye may be the children of your Father which is in heaven ; for He maketh His sun to rise on the evil and on the good, and sendeth rain on the just and on the unjust."

Truly the "Law of Love." That those of your readers who are familiar with Greek may judge the original MS. for themselves, I here submit a *half-size photograph* of what I obtained. (See p. 74.)

I close without comment, merely reminding your readers: That this sitting was held in the light.

That the sheet of note paper remained in my possession from the time I first received and examined it till the close of the sitting ; and has never been out of my possession since.

That, for the reality of the phenomena I had the evidence of two senses : that of feeling, and best and most convincing of all, the testimony of what the old poet calls the "faithful eyes."

New York, Oct. 15th, 1876.

The other case is recorded in the *Spiritualist* of Dec. 1, 1876, and Mr. Blackburn's attestation supplies all the necessary information :—

The writing in the accompanying cut is a fac-simile of that which was obtained upon one of Dr. Slade's slates in the presence of Mr. Charles Blackburn of Parkfield, Didsbury, near Manchester. Mr. Blackburn states that in broad daylight a crumb of pencil was placed on the top of the table, and a clean slate turned face downwards over the pencil. The four sitters, including Dr. Slade, then joined their hands, with the exception that Dr. Slade placed one of his hands

Matth. 6: 9–13.

ΠΑΤΗΡ ἡμῶν ὁ ἐν τοῖς οὐρανοῖς· ἁγιασθήτω τὸ ὄνομά σου· ἐλθέτω ἡ βασιλεία σου· γενηθήτω τὸ θέλημά σου, ὡς ἐν οὐρανῷ καὶ ἐπὶ τῆς γῆς. Τὸν ἄρτον ἡμῶν τὸν ἐπιούσιον δὸς ἡμῖν σήμερον. καὶ ἄφες ἡμῖν τὰ ὀφειλήματα ἡμῶν, ὡς καὶ ἡμεῖς ἀφίεμεν τοῖς ὀφειλέταις ἡμῶν, καὶ μὴ εἰσενέγκῃς ἡμᾶς εἰς πειρασμόν, ἀλλὰ ῥῦσαι ἡμᾶς ἀπὸ τοῦ πονηροῦ. ὅτι σοῦ ἐστιν ἡ βασιλεία καὶ ἡ δύναμις, καὶ ἡ δόξα, εἰς τοὺς αἰῶνας ἀμήν. –|

K.S.

upon the top of one corner of the slate, whilst Miss Cook, at the other end of the chain of sitters, placed one of her hands upon the opposite corner. Dr. Slade sat sideways, and his feet were in sight all the time. Soon they heard the pencil hard at work, and the message seemed to be a long one, for the writing could be heard going on for five or six minutes; then it ceased, and raps came upon the table. The slate was turned up and found to be full of Greek writing. Mr. Blackburn wrapped up the slate in his handkerchief, and carried it to the rooms of the National Association of Spiritualists, where it is now framed under glass, and is on public view. The writing is the dry dusty writing of slate pencil. The sitters were Mr. Charles Blackburn, Mrs. Henry Cook, of Hackney, Miss Kate S. Cook, and Dr. Slade.

Another specimen of Greek was obtained by Mr. Gledstanes, who also had some Arabic and English writing on the same slate. He went to Slade, I may say, with the desire and hope of getting some French message, which he might give to M. Leymarie in Paris, a city in which Mr. Gledstanes had for some time been resident. The remarks which I have before made as to the difference in handwritings find an illustration here. The Greek writings obtained by Messrs. Owen and Blackburn are identical in type, and seem to me to be hastily written, as if by a hand familiar with the character, and accustomed to write it *currente calamo*. The letters are not laboriously formed, as would be the case if they were copied by one who was ignorant of the language. The characters on the slates of Messrs. Gledstanes and Wedgwood are entirely different—are, in my opinion, formed by another hand— and are signed alike, but differently from the other writings. These points have their obvious bearing on the question of the separate nature of the Intelligence, and also of the reality of the phenomenon.

Since Slade has been on the Continent, at the Hague and Berlin, we find that messages in Dutch and German are written. Canon X. Mouls, with Slade in Belgium, obtained writing in French, a language with which he was probably most familiar, as well as in English, the language of the Psychic.

In London one gentleman obtained writing in both Spanish and Portuguese, though neither he nor any person in the room knew a word of either language. In an adjoining room, however, it is curious to note that there was a gentleman, Dr. Carter Blake, who knows both. It is right, however, to notice that during the time when the experiment was being made, Dr. Blake was in conversation about other subjects. The matter of the message, he tells me, is quite unlike anything that would have been in his mind. He has no pretensions to be a good Portuguese scholar; never uses the language for thought or word, except in the way of business, though he knows Spanish well.

The same results are got with Watkins, in America. Madame H. P. Blavatsky, a Russian lady now resident in New York, and author of *Isis Unveiled*, went to Watkins, and having written among other names, on separate pieces of paper, one in Russian character, she was asked by the Psychic to allow it to be written on the slate, as it was too difficult for him to pronounce. Madame Blavatsky placed her hand alone on a slate, under which a fragment of pencil had been placed. Mr. Watkins did not touch the slate. "An instant after, on turning up the slate, the appellation, consisting of three names, was found written in full, and in Russian characters, with this curious exception, that one or two letters were exchanged for those of Latin character, having the same phonetic value; *e.g.* an *f*, pronounced in Russian *v*, but written *b*, was substituted for the latter letter."

Again, a teacher of the Greek language in the Collegiate Institute, Springfield, Massachusetts, United States of America, Mr. T. T. Timayenis, a modern Greek by birth, obtained from Watkins, in original characters of Romaic, "the name of his grandfather, and three lines of Greek words, correctly spelled, and with accents and breathings correctly placed." To this he testifies in his own name, and, moreover, states that the "name written is very peculiar, almost unpronounceable by English lips. The slate was in full view throughout, and Watkins merely touched one corner with a motionless finger."

The same Psychic has recently obtained writing in correct and properly formed Chinese characters. It is probable that Psychography could be obtained in any given language, provided a person were present who understood that language even slightly. And there is some evidence which goes to prove that on rare occasions a language is used with which no person present is familiar; just as, far more certainly, facts are given which are not known to any one in the room.

It is, however, very desirable that extended experiment should be made in this direction before any definite opinion is formed.

III.

SPECIAL TESTS, SHOWING THE IMPOSSIBILITY OF PREVIOUS PREPARATION OF THE WRITING.

BEYOND the evidence obtained by the senses of the observer, and from the fact that the subject-matter of the communications frequently contains what the Psychic could not be supposed to know, as well as from the fact that the language in which it is conveyed is one with which he is not familiar, there are additional tests which go still further to show the impossibility of previous preparation for purposes of deception.

It must be borne in mind that these writings are not obtained solely by professional Psychics, who, having an interest in procuring them for money, may be supposed to be under some temptation to manufacture a counterfeit when the real article is not forthcoming. They are of frequent, not to say regular occurrence in families into which no professional aid ever is admitted, when the matter of the writing is of so private a nature usually as to be held sacred, and where publicity is neither asked nor tolerated. Such cases form a very large factor in a fair argument on this question.

And in this connexion I am concerned to say again that the so-called exposure of the *modus operandi* of a professional Psychic by a professional conjurer is of so little importance as to be practically *nihil ad rem*. Mr. Maskelyne, on his own stage, surrounded by his own confederates, and using his own prepared apparatus, does something which burlesques the results obtained by Slade. What then? If the imitation were moderately good, it would be a creditable counterfeit, such as the skilful illusionist should have no difficulty in producing on his own terms. The stage thunder, the stage dinner, the false sovereign, the mask and wig of the actor, may all be made more or less like the reality which they counterfeit. Mr. Maskelyne's is a sorry piece of illusion, unworthy one who passes as so great an artist, and only excusable because he finds it good enough for his method of misguiding a credulous public. But were it never so good, what would it prove? Simply that a thing can be imitated when unlimited means of so doing are provided. That is hardly a point that we need to have demonstrated; and if those who lay stress upon it find any comfort in that demonstration they are welcome to it. If, however, they flatter themselves that it extends any further, then they must be advised to commence the study of logic.

Furthermore, let it be remembered that the conjurer is a man who has devoted special faculties, specially trained, to the development of his art. His nimble fingers have gone through many a weary lesson before they have enabled him to do what he does. The

Psychic, as often as not, is a lady or gentleman, a boy, or even a child, who could not perform a Maskelyne trick to save his or her life, and who has usually as little knowledge of the method by which the results are obtained as my reader probably has. It is Nature *versus* Art; and in this, as in all other cases, though Art may copy, it cannot rival Nature.

A great deal is made too, and quite naturally, of the tricks that can be played in the dark, when a trained and practised trickster has full liberty for his pranks. As I write there lies before me this week's *Academy* (Jan. 5, 1878), in which a review of *Houdin's Conjuring* is made the vehicle for a long story of the method of imposture used on a certain occasion (not specified) by a Psychic (not named) at a time and place (not particularised) in Cambridge. This is, most unfairly, turned into a sort of illustration of the way in which Slade managed his business. The critic, who evidently knows nothing of the subject, must prepare himself to answer such cases as those adduced here before his attacks will have much weight. As a matter of fact, no case is here recorded which took place in darkness; none where any such imposture as he relies upon was possible; none where the critic can fairly say that every reasonable precaution was not taken to insure fair and straightforward dealing.

I reiterate the fact that, when these experiments are made in public, they are made under rigid conditions which preclude deception. Men familiar with the phenomena, and who are not scared or driven off their balance by their occurrence, subject them to repeated observation, and evoke them under carefully prescribed conditions. They are not content to leave a conjurer's license to the Psychic, but compel him to attempt his experiment under conditions which render it absolutely sure that all is straightforward, and which frequently are so rigid as to make success all but impossible. Under these conditions many of the experiments quoted in this treatise have been conducted, and I claim to advance my argument a step further by referring here to some of the most conspicuous.

I have already recorded that Watkins has submitted himself to the careful testing of a committee, in a strange hall, and with slates which he had never even seen. Under these circumstances fifty words were written. This is a fair instance of the difference between the *modus operandi* of the true Psychic, and the method of the conjurer.

In a similar manner Slade, when in London, voluntarily came from his own rooms to those of the British Association of Spiritualists, 38 Great Russell Street, and submitted himself to test by a committee specially selected from the members of that association, and permanently organised for the purpose of conducting scientific research into Psychic phenomena. He made no other condition save this. He requested that the committee should experiment with him by twos, as he had found by experience that the best results are obtained when the number of persons present is small. He was willing to use the table and slates provided by the committee, and made no stipulation whatever as to who the observers should be, or in what order or manner they tested his powers.

From the carefully-recorded minutes of the committee I extract the reports of Mr. Desmond Fitz-Gerald, M.S.Tel.E., and Mr. J. W. Gray, C.E.; of Mr. George King, and Dr. Carter Blake, Doc. Sci.; and of Mr. T. H. Edmands and Mr. Hannah.

REPORT OF MR. DESMOND FITZ-GERALD, M.S.TEL.E., AND MR. J. W. GRAY, C.E.

We sat down to an ordinary deal, double-flap, Pembroke table. Dr. Slade sat with a flap to right and left, but sideways, so that his legs did not pass under the table. Mr. Fitz-Gerald sat on his right, opposite the flap, and Mr. Gray opposite to Dr. Slade. All joined hands on the top of the table, and at about the middle thereof. Raps, and even blows, were then almost immediately heard and felt beneath the table, these being sufficiently strong to cause the table to vibrate distinctly; and in this way was affirmatively answered the question, "Will you write?" Dr. Slade then bit off a small piece of pencil and placed it on a slate, the frame of which bore a mark, so that the slate could not be turned over without detection. The slate was then passed several times partially under the table and withdrawn by Dr. Slade, who held it by one corner, his other hand joining that of the other sitters on the top of the table. At no time was the slate in such a position that the writing could by any possibility have been done by Dr. Slade. After a few of these movements of the slate, and whilst it was partially visible, and apparently close against the table, both Dr. Slade's hands being full in view, a sound as of writing on the slate was distinctly heard, and then, after it had moved three times against the table (to indicate that the writing was finished), the slate was withdrawn, and writing was found thereon, extending right across the slate, lengthwise.

The next experiment was with a folding slate, which had

been bought by Mr. Fitz-Gerald for the purpose. A crumb of pencil having been placed on one leaf of the slate, and the other leaf folded over it, Dr. Slade took hold of the closed slate between the thumb and forefinger of the right hand, and placed his other hand on those of the other sitters, on the top of the table. The slate was then passed several times beneath the table for the fraction of a second, and was then held by Dr. Slade above the table, in which position writing was distinctly heard on it, Mr. Fitz-Gerald placing his ear close to the slate to make quite sure of this fact. On the slate being then opened, writing was found on one leaf thereof, the words being: "He is not a developing medium;" this being evidently a reply to a remark made by Dr. Slade, a minute or so before, that Mr. Gray was a strong medium. The slates being then removed from the table, we placed our hands on the latter, and Dr. Slade asked that it might be raised. After being strongly tilted once or twice, it was suddenly raised from the floor, and turned over above our heads. The latter movement was so sudden, however, that the exact conditions immediately before it occurred had not been noted. It was therefore suggested that the experiment should be tried whether the table could be made to rise slowly and vertically whilst under careful observation. The request that it should do so was immediately acceded to. The medium placed one foot right away from the table, so that it was well in view of the sitters, and the other foot he placed beneath one of Mr. Fitz-Gerald's, while all hands were joined on the top of the table. It then, and under the closest observation, rose twice about six inches from the ground, the top remaining perfectly horizontal during the movements. Thus ended a most satisfactory séance.

(Signed) JOHN WM. GRAY.

I fully concur in the above account.

DESMOND G. FITZ-GERALD.

REPORT OF MR. GEORGE KING AND DR. CARTER BLAKE.

Dr. Slade having kindly volunteered to give a séance to the members of the Experimental Research Committee, we assembled to meet him this evening. We gathered in the large séance room, and while waiting proceeded with the routine business of the committee. At about seven o'clock Dr. Slade arrived, and sat for a little chatting with us. He said he could not that evening sit with more than two at a time, and as there were about eight of us, we drew lots for the order of precedence. My lot fell to be in the third couple, and my partner was Dr. Carter Blake. The previous sitters were with the medium about twenty minutes, and experienced some strong physical manifestations, for when Dr. C. Blake and I entered the small séance room we found that one globe of the gaselier had been broken, we were told, by the table having been violently tossed up into the air.

Dr. Slade, Dr. Blake, and I sat down at a small and very rough table belonging to Dr. Carter Blake. My companions sat facing each other at opposite sides of the table, and I sat between them at the medium's right, and thus, as he always held the slate in his right hand when he placed it under the table, I had every opportunity of closely observing him. We used two slates, supplied by a member of the committee, one an ordinary school slate, the other a folding book-slate. We had a number of very short messages, sometimes on one slate, sometimes on the other, obtained in the way which has been so often described. Usually the slates were completely hidden under the table, and thus the séance was not so conclusive as the private one I had had with the same medium a week or two before. I observed a mark on the school slate, which, on these occasions when the slate was not passed entirely out of sight, enabled me to say positively that the writing was done on the *upper* side of the slate, and not on the under. One little circumstance seems to me very remarkable, and I am astonished that attention has not been more forcibly called to it in accounts of séances with Dr. Slade. [*Note A.*] The crumb of pencil invariably remains at the point where it stops after writing the message, forming a perfect continuation of the last stroke of the last letter. This fact, trifling in itself, to my mind goes far to prove that the message had been written with that identical piece of pencil, and on the upper side of the slate. I do not see how otherwise the medium could place it in position with such mathematical accuracy. It may also be thought worthy of record that the style of the handwriting was very dissimilar from that of the message I had received at the private séance above referred to, and that the intelligence purporting to communicate was different also. [*Note B.*]

Dr. Slade afterwards took an ordinary blacklead pencil, about six inches in length, and laid it on the slate above a half sheet of note paper which I had supplied. He passed them under the table, when the pencil appeared to drop on the ground. We immediately looked for it, but could nowhere find it. Dr. Slade then passed the slate with a crumb of slate pencil on it under the table, and asked where the blacklead pencil had been put. The written answer was, "On the top of the door;" and on the top of the door Dr. Blake found it. The door was about ten feet from where we sat, and none of us had stirred from our chairs from the moment of entering the room. The incident was a curious one; but as I had not the means of identifying the pencil, and had not searched the top of the door before beginning the séance, it does not carry very great weight. [*Note C.*]

GEO. KING.

Note A.—Attention has been often drawn to this point in communications which have appeared in the *The Spiritualist* newspaper.—C. C. B.

Note B.—The handwriting was dissimilar from that of "Allie," "Phœbe," and purported to be that of "Owossoo."—C. C. B.

Note C.—The pencil found by me on the lintel of the door was identified by me by certain marks as the same pencil placed by Dr. Slade on the paper, and subsequently dropped. It ought to be stated that my own chair was dragged from beneath me by a force acting on the other side of the room to that on which Dr. Slade sat; and that I was forcibly touched on the shoulder under like conditions. With these additions I coincide in Mr. G. King's report.—C. CARTER BLAKE.

REPORTS OF MR. T. H. EDMANDS AND MR. R. HANNAH.

Dr. Slade attended the meeting of the Research Committee, and, after a short interval, was shown into the front séance room, where he received the members by twos. Mr.

R. Hannah and I were the last to enter. We found Dr. Slade standing by a common deal table, which, with the three chairs to be occupied by us, was detached by an interval of eight or ten feet from the other articles in the room. I received the slates which were used, one a double-folding, and the other a common school slate, from the members who had entered immediately preceding Mr. Hannah and myself, and took them into the séance room. On the common slate a short message was written whilst it was partially under the table. I then expressed a wish that something might be written in my pocket-book, which I handed to Dr. Slade, with a small bit of my own pencil (blue). We were informed that a trial would be made to give us a message. Dr. Slade held the pocket book over the table, open and in full view, then dropped the bit of pencil on the open leaf, then turned over the half cover so as to close the book, except so far as was prevented by Dr. Slade's thumb being at one corner holding the book. In about a minute, without any action or movement by Dr. Slade, writing was heard to be in progress, the whole book being still in sight, as also were both hands of Dr. Slade, one only being used to hold the book, and a message was written.

A small piece of pencil was then placed on one side of the double slate, and the other side closed over it. The closed slate was then held for an instant by Dr. Slade, partly under the table, but at Mr. Hannah's suggestion, it was put on the top of the table, and pressed down with the tips of Dr. Slade's fingers and thumb. When the slate was brought up and placed on the top of the table, Dr. Slade opened it to show that it was then free from writing. Almost instantly writing was heard, and on opening the slate a sentence was found to be written, which was preserved, and attested by Mr. Hannah and myself by our signatures on the frame of the slate, and the slate handed to Mr. Fitz-Gerald, to whom it belonged. Mr. Hannah is of opinion that no more satisfactory conditions could be required as proof, that Dr. Slade had no active part in producing the writings, than were afforded by these two experiments with the pocket-book and the slate, and I concur with him entirely.

T. H. EDMANDS.

A series of sittings was given by Dr. Slade to the Research Committee at 38, Great Russell Street, on the 15th December. He was shown into the front séance room, where he received the members by twos.

Mr. Edmands and I were the last to enter, and we found Dr. Slade standing by a bare table, which, with the three chairs to be occupied by us, was detached by an interval of eight or ten feet from the other articles in the room.

Mr. Edmands took into the room the slates to be experimented upon, one a double-folding, and the other a common school slate.

On this common slate a short message was written whilst it was partially under the table. Mr. Edmands then expressed a wish that something might be written in his pocket-book. A very small portion of prepared lead was placed upon it, and Dr. Slade held it, quite open, in sight, but partly covered by the corner of the flap of the table. In about a minute the book seemed to shut without any action on the part of Dr. Slade, and writing was heard to be in progress, the whole book being then in sight, as also were both of Dr. Slade's hands.

A small piece of pencil was then placed on one side of the double slate, and the other side closed down over it. The closed slate was then held for an instant by Dr. Slade, partly under the table, but at my suggestion he put it on the top of the table, and pressed it down with the tips of his fingers and thumb. Almost instantly writing was heard, and on opening the slate a sentence was found, which was preserved, and afterwards attested by Mr. Edmands and myself signing our names on the frame.

I do not think more satisfactory conditions could be required as proof that Dr. Slade had no active part in producing the writing than were afforded by these two experiments with the pocket-book and the folding slate.

An incident attracted my notice during the sitting which I may be allowed to mention, as it bears on a part of the evidence given in the prosecution, where it was said that Dr. Slade adopted the rather uncouth mode of biting off bits of pencil in order that he might have some pretext for the noise made by "clearing his throat." The only time during the sitting Dr. Slade indulged in this "knack" was when holding the pocket-book open partly under the table. He had not hitherto bitten a pencil at all, as the sentence on the common slate was written with a largish piece, which had been on the table. The knack seemed spasmodic, or as indicating that he might be in very slight degree in the state which is called "under control." Besides these writings, certain unimportant movements of the table occurred.

R. HANNAH.

In the course of this report occurs the name of a scientific gentleman who had great opportunity of observing the phenomena which occurred in Slade's presence, and who has left us a very exact record of some of his observations. Mr. Carter Blake, Doctor of Science, late secretary to the Anthropological Society of Great Britain, and now lecturer on comparative anatomy at Westminster Hospital, is the observer, and his records, beside giving facts, note also some deductions bearing on the source and operation of the force to which I shall have occasion to recur hereafter.

On Monday, the 8th instant, I had the pleasure of visiting Dr. Slade. The manifestations were of the same kind as those described by many of your correspondents. I was struck with the fact that the motive power which pulled at my coat, took a slate from my hand, and carried it under the table, proceeded from my right hand, while Dr. Slade was on my left. The message given on the slate was of the usual character from "Allie." Subsequently, the initials of a deceased person known to myself were written on the slate when the side was turned downwards, and quite invisible to Dr. Slade. Afterwards some writing was obtained on the slate from the same assumed source, the meaning of which was intelligible to myself, and not to Dr. Slade. Hands were seen, and my coat forcibly pulled by some other force than his own. The table was raised up when both his hands, and both mine, were on it, and my feet on his. No motion of his feet could have done this. He then leaving the table, it forcibly threw itself in my lap, and subsequently, in a reversed position, on my head. The accordion was played when held by one of Dr. Slade's hands.

The hands shown near me cast a distinct shadow, produced by the sunlight on the table, and on my white waistcoat.

The effect on my mind was the certainty of Dr. Slade's perfect good faith in the matter, and the conviction that the force which produced these singular conditions was intelligent, and acted from a spot or spots separate from the medium.

On Sunday, September 10, 1876, after mass, I visited Dr. Slade at 9·40 a.m., and found him in good health and spirits. Stepping into the back drawing-room, the table, which was covered, had the cloth removed, and the cloth as well as the table were most minutely inspected by me, as had been the carpet on a previous occasion. Dr. Slade sat at the west side of the table, and I at the south. I do not think it necessary in any way further to describe the table than by saying it is of good solid ash, and the carpentry with which it is made is good. The "strut" or "bracket," which may be used to support either of the flaps of the table, is precisely similar to that in a deal table which I have in my own possession. There is, in fact, nothing abnormal or unusual about this arrangement, which I only mention because attention had been drawn to it with a view to infer that there was something suspicious. The chairs around the table (which do not belong to Dr. Slade) are ordinary cane-bottom chairs, are not connected with any mechanism either under the carpet, to the ceiling, or in any way whatever. The chair which I will call A was placed by me, after inspection, at the north-east corner of the table, its front face being diagonal with the north side of the table. Another chair (B) was placed in full view of myself, parallel with the eastern face of the table.

Dr. Slade had on French pumps, and his dress was "of the period." I had on heavy side-spring walking boots. Dr. Slade, with a view to show that it was perfectly impossible for him to produce any motion of or under the table by his feet, attempted to sit sideways with one of his feet on a chair moved to the south-west corner of the table between us. Failing to be able to sit comfortably in this way, he placed his feet at a distance of about six inches (minimum distance) from the south-west corner of the table. I took off my own boots and placed them behind my chair at the spot marked F, where they could not be touched by any one but myself, and only by my right hand. A sofa was behind me, and the boots were partially underneath this sofa.

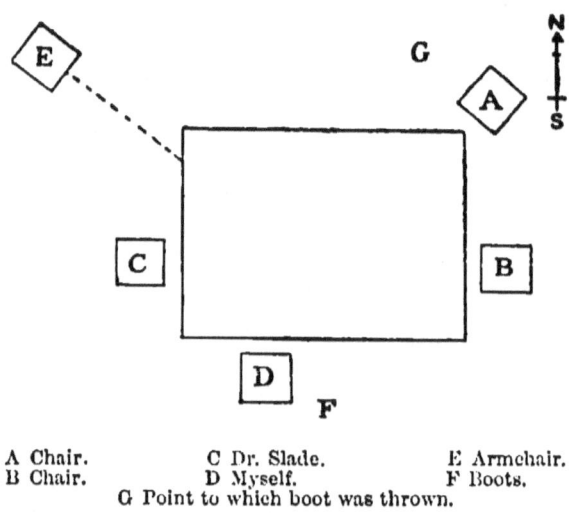

A Chair.   C Dr. Slade.   E Armchair.
B Chair.   D Myself.   F Boots.
G Point to which boot was thrown.

I then placed my feet on those of Dr. Slade, and rendered any action on the part of his feet impossible. The slate was then held by him under the table, as already described by Serjeant Cox, and some twenty others, with perfect accuracy. I do not think it necessary to say more than that on the present occasion my attention was chiefly directed to *constater* the fact that both sides of the slate were carefully examined by me and ascertained not to have any prepared writing or marking. Dr. Slade permitted me to hold the slate in my own hands and turn either side up. The pencil crumb was soon heard writing, and the following message produced on the upper surface of the slate:—

Dear Sir,—I present my compliments, and wish you to say Wm. Trippen [or Tuppen] came, and wishes his friends to know he can return. I left earth Aug. 16th, at No. 1, Thomas's Cottage, Bournewalk, Butler, age 68.
                                                                                Wm. T.

The meaning of the above is perfectly unintelligible to me. While it was being written, Dr. Slade was carrying on a conversation on another subject.

We then proceeded with the séance.

Whilst waiting for the next manifestation, I noticed a condition which I had not previously observed with Dr. Slade. His hands being on both mine, in the centre of the table, the muscles of my forearms were seized with a convulsive motion, and the waves of this motion, according to my impression, proceeded from my elbows to the finger tips, and not the converse, as some persons might be led to expect. The sensation was unlike that which would have been produced by an electric battery under the table, and was more like what I should imagine was the sensation of the *aura epileptica*. Of course I have not the slightest pretensions to the abnormal condition which is called, for reasons unknown to me, "mediumistic," a badly-constructed word, which has apparently been coined on as absurd a model as "ritualistic."

The chair marked A then rose to a distance of nine inches from the ground, preserving its parallelism with the floor, and fell with a violent blow. The arm-chair, E, in the corner of the room, was slid on its castors in the direction of the dotted line in the sketch. My right boot was violently thrown over my head in the air to the point marked G. I requested that the other boot should be placed gently on the chair B, but before the words were out of my mouth it was thrown on the table, striking the hands of Dr. Slade and myself, and producing slight excoriation in his case, and ecchymosis in mine. During all this time his hands were on mine on the table, and my feet on his. No possible motion of any part of his body could have produced any of these effects. The distance between the leg of the chair A and his toe, if the latter had been outstretched, was found to be sixteen inches. The distance between him in his chair and the spot where I had placed the boots was three feet four inches, and that from the spot where the boots were to the spot where one of them fell was seven feet three inches, a curved trajectory being added, so as to allow for my height in the chair. I should estimate the line of trajectory at twelve feet. The table was afterwards raised, and thrown in a reversed position on my head.

In the evening I had another séance with Dr. Slade, at which was present a celebrated anatomist, who was satisfied of the *bonâ fide* character of the manifestations. I was struck with the identity in so many cases of the phenomena. Both at this and at the previous séance short messages were written by a long pencil—six inches in length—held about nine inches under the table. The public may be amused with the statement that such pencils are invariably rejected by Dr. Slade's controls.

I must quote the evidence of the Rev. John Page Hopps, editor of *The Truthseeker*, principally because his report shows that he went to Slade with a mind possessed of the various allegations which had been made against him. The usual conditions obtained, and the slate, having been first held by Slade in order to inquire whether anything could be done, was then held in order to put the question, whether writing could be produced so as to fill the slate. To this query the reply, "We will do so soon," was given, *the pencil lying at the end of the last letter.* Mr. Page Hopps then proceeds :—

The slate was again put under, and then for about three minutes I heard writing. When the sounds ceased, the slate was carefully withdrawn (in this, as in every case, flat as it had lain during the writing). The slate was completely filled with the following "message," addressed, I presume, to me :—

DEAR SIR,—God's will be done on earth, as it is done in heaven: that the Christ-principle of doing good be inculcated as the only saving efficacy from selfishness, discord, and error; not simply to be investigated, but unfolded; not to be obtained by formal rites, but because originally implanted, must necessarily be developed in the everlasting life of man, and it only remains for man to place himself under the conditions of harmony to become receptive to the wide-spreading volume of God's universal welcome.—A. W. SLADE.

It may be said that this slate was written already, and adroitly changed; but further on it will be seen that I got, without waiting, a similar slateful on my own marked slate, only produced by me just before the writing occurred.

I had heard of suspicious delays, movements, and noises, elaborate breaking of pencil, throat sounds, and the like. I was astonished at the ease, simplicity, and quiet of the whole thing. I had heard of the slate being detained on Dr. Slade's knees, or disappearing. More than once I saw it at once put under the table, with its top pressed close under the top of the table, and one side of the frame well seen the whole time. I had heard of the writing being done before the slate went into position; I, on each occasion that the writing was produced, heard all the sounds of writing on a slate I had seen was blank. I had heard of the slates being changed; I can only say that, after the sounds of writing were heard by me, the slate was very slowly withdrawn, and, in each case, the pencil lay precisely at the end of the last word. I had heard of the writing being done by Dr. Slade's finger, armed with a tiny grain of pencil, but one of his hands lay on mine upon the table, while part of the other, holding the slate, was in view the whole time, and it never stirred during the writing which I heard, and which on one occasion covered the whole of a moderate-sized slate. I had heard of sympathetic ink and the like; the slate we used was a new one, perfectly grey; the pencil was a soft slate pencil, and the whole of the writing which I examined, was composed of dry pencil dust. I had heard of doubts whether the writing was done on the top or the under side of the slate; in my case I am certain the writing was done on the side between the slate and the table.

Two days after, I saw Dr. Slade again. On this occasion I took two new-framed slates, which I marked. I particularly asked whether it was not possible to get writing without putting the slate under the table, and was told it was quite possible. My two slates were then laid upon the table, with a tiny bit of pencil between; and upon them in the full daylight we laid our four hands. I then distinctly heard the sound of writing, and, on lifting up the top slate, found these words written, but very badly:—"We cannot give you a communication, only a proof our power." I remarked that though one or two words (the word "communication," for instance) were very badly written, Dr. Slade at once read them. On my way from Dr. Slade's this slate got broken to splinters—how, I know not; so I returned the next day to try another, again taking two marked framed slates. A first "message" procured under the table as on the first day, but with more agitation of the hand, told me that "they" had broken my slate, because they wanted to give me more! Anyhow, the result was remarkable. My first slate, held by Dr. Slade, was somehow smashed to atoms, only about two inches remaining in one corner of it. The second I laid on the top of the table, a bit of pencil was put under it, and our hands were then put on or near it. The writing was then heard, and in about three minutes ceased, when, on lifting the slate, this "message" was found, well written, in regular lines, and covering the slate :—

The spirit of truth, which Jesus prophesied would come in these days of the age of war and force, is that undivided fraternising spirit of all love and goodness that unites the redeemed souls on earth and in heaven into one grand brotherhood of God—to open the way for the coming of this spirit has been the work of mediums—now may they have the strength given them to go on with the good work. A. W. SLADE.

I have the slate in my study now. It has on it my private mark.

The following account, drawn up by the editor of the *Spiritualist*, and published in that journal, records a remarkable duplication of a message, as well as the production of the original message on slates which were never out of sight of the observers :—

A few days ago Mr. Charles Blackburn, of Parkfield,

Didsbury, near Manchester, came to London, and invited two thorough disbelievers in Spiritualism, both of them influential men of business well known in the city, to a séance with Dr. Slade. They visited him at 8, Upper Bedford Place on Monday last week, between three and four o'clock in the afternoon. Mr. Blackburn brought with him a slate purchased in Manchester. It was a folding slate—that is to say, it had hinges on the back, and when it was closed the two slates faced each other; the outside case was of wood. A private mark was put upon this slate by a friend of Mr. Blackburn's in Manchester; and a London partner of the gentleman who had made that mark was one of those who attended the séance to watch the results.

The two London gentlemen took the slate into the séance room, and as they held it open, Dr. Slade dropped a piece of pencil upon it, about the size of a grain of wheat. They then tied a string tightly round the slate, after which one of them laid it upon the table, placed his elbow upon it. Writing was heard. They then took the slate into the next room, opened it in the presence of Mr. and Miss Blackburn and Mr. Simmons, and *both leaves of the slate were found to be covered with the dry dusty writing of slate pencil.* The crumb of pencil had been somewhat worn in the production of the writing. *From first to last the slate never went out of sight of its owners.* The séance took place in broad daylight.

Two or three words were spelt wrongly in the message. So after it had been examined, Dr. Slade washed it off, and the pencil was placed in it again to get more writing under the same conditions. A noise inside the slate like that of writing was heard, and the gentlemen took the slate away for the purpose of opening it at one of their offices. After they had left the house, Dr. Slade passed into a trance, and the communicating intelligence told Mr. Simmons that the sitters had not waited long enough; there was no writing on the slate; the spirits had been rolling the pencil about, trying to take hold of it. This afterwards proved to be the case.

Next day they accordingly came again at 2.30 p.m., and obtained writing under the same conditions as at the first sitting. After they left the séance room, and before they untied the slate, Mr. Blackburn had a sitting with Dr. Slade, and asked whether there were any writing on the slate this time. The spirits said they would write a duplicate of the message on another slate. This was done while the slate, with a crumb of pencil on it, was held by Dr. Slade flat against the under side of the table. His face was to the light. Mr. Blackburn had previously cleaned the slate himself. He took the message into the next room, the string of the folding slate was cut, and the messages on the two slates were found to be identical, with the exception that the one on the folding slate contained an additional paragraph.

This account is drawn up from testimony given to us by Mr. Blackburn, Mr. Simmons, and Dr. Slade.

And this satisfactory method of endeavouring to obtain writing on the investigator's own slate was successful in the case of Mr. J. Seaman, well known in the newspaper world, who writes from 11 Southampton Street, Strand, and who, primed (as in a case above noted) with all that suspicion could instil, obtained what convinced him of the *bonâ fides* of Slade, and of the reality of his power :—

On Friday morning last, the 1st inst., at about noon, I called, with my friend, Dr. Carter Blake, at 8 Upper Bedford Place, and was introduced to Dr. Slade, who was quietly chatting with Mr. Simmons and another gentleman in the drawing-room—the room which will go down to posterity as the apartment where Simmons "winked" and "pumped the visitors." I found Mr. Simmons without his "wink," but he certainly "pumped me," for as he politely asked me to remove my overcoat, he ascertained from my answer that I was only wearing one. But no use was made of this discovery by him. Dr. Slade, who took me into the back room, did not sit with his back to the window, but full in the light. He never once rested the slate (my own) on his knee, but held it in such a manner that I saw quite one-third of it, and his thumb the whole of the time. His arm did not move "as in the manner of writing," and was only moved when the slate was placed nearer to me, or on my head. The tendons of his wrist were perfectly motionless, and the writing was not curved. It consisted of four distinct messages:—

    (a) Eight words in one straight line.
    (b) Twelve   ,,   three   ,,
    (c) Three   ,,   one   ,,
    (d) Six   ,,   two   ,,

The lines for the most part extended parallel with the longer side, and right across a twelve-inch framed ordinary school slate. All the messages were written on the top side of the slate, which I had previously marked "top" and "bottom," to distinguish the two surfaces. Of this I am as certain as I am of my own existence. My attention was not attempted to be directed to a supposed light on my elbow, though I confess I diverted Dr. Slade's attention to a picture on the wall, the subject of which was familiar to me, with a view to see if he would attempt to write or do anything else when he fancied I was off my guard. We conversed the whole time. Raps were heard from many parts of the room and furniture. The table was lifted evenly from the floor, while I held Dr. Slade's hands with my hands, and guarded his feet with my feet. Had he used his knees (which were plainly in sight), the table would have tilted, rather than have been raised easily. A bell placed under the table, out of reach, but in my sight, was rung while Dr. Slade was standing up, and then rapidly lifted from the ground, moved towards my left to above the level of the table, and then violently hurled between us towards my right, and fell with a crash on the extreme right of the table, thus describing nearly a circle. I was touched on the right hip, which was too far off to be reached by Dr. Slade's feet (always in view). In my sitting position at that moment, first my right leg and then the leg of the table were, as it were, guarding my right side from any attack from where Dr. Slade sat. The "force" was evidently behind me on my right. Confirmatory of that view, the chair on which I sat, and while I sat on it, was suddenly pushed from behind towards the table and towards Dr. Slade, whose white and red striped socks and French pumps were visible in their natural position. I say pushed in preference to pulled, because the sensation was of some one behind my chair. I looked round to see who or what was there. Where I sat before this pushing was quite out of radius for Dr. Slade's outstretched foot to hook me and the chair towards him. I have seen too many conjurers, and performed too many sleight-of-hand tricks myself, not to know when the critical moment arrives for the success of the trick in hand; but at this sitting I saw no evidence of trickery of any kind. I leave to others to explain the phenomena. I can only say that I am convinced the writing was on the top side of the slate, on which alone Dr. Slade's thumb (always full in view) rested; when the writing was produced on the slate, as it rested on my head, the knuckles of his hand were pressed against my temples, and while there, no movement of Dr. Slade's fingers took place. Dr. Slade was suffering in bodily health during my visit, and expressed himself satisfied with the results of the sitting. Not one word was said about spirits while I remained at 8 Upper Bedford Place.

11 Southampton Street, Strand,
London, W.C.

WRITING WITHIN SLATES SECURELY SCREWED TOGETHER.

Mrs. Louisa Andrews, 66 Spring Street, Springfield, Massachusetts, U.S.A., a valued correspondent of my own, testifies to obtaining writing under conditions, if possible, even more stringent. She obtained a message in answer to one written by herself inside a slate, which she had tightly screwed together.

During my stay of over two months in the house with Dr. Slade last summer, I took a folding-slate into my bed-room, and with it a screw and a screw-driver—having previously had screw-holes made in both frames. On one of the inner sides of this double slate I wrote a few lines, addressed to a friend in spirit-life, after which I placed a fragment of pencil within, and fastened the two leaves securely together.

In this condition I took it down stairs, and placed it on the top of the table at which the medium was seated. Almost immediately we heard the scratching sound made by the pencil in writing; and after the seance was over, on opening the slate (which I did not do in the presence of the medium, but after returning to my room, where I had left the screw-driver), I found a reply to what I had written, signed with the Christian name of the spirit whom I had addressed—whether written by this spirit or not I cannot say, and any opinion I might form on that point would be worthless except to myself. What I *know* is, that some power caused writing to be done on the inner side of a folding-slate, which did not leave my possession, and which remained firmly screwed together till I unfastened it.

Nor is this experiment unique. The same result is recorded as having been obtained by the presence of one William Petty, of Newcastle-on-Tyne. Mr. John Mould, of 12 St. Thomas's Crescent, Newcastle, of the firm of J. Mould & Co., corn-factors, thus writes under date December 22, 1876:—

I have been holding sittings with William Petty *in my own house* for slate-writing, on a folding-slate, *tightly screwed together*, and I have had several most successful seances, but the most conclusive obtained was on Wednesday night, when I put a sheet of my own note-paper between the slates, *screwed them together*, and, after sitting ten minutes, I unscrewed the slate and found a side face drawn on the paper, with a message written below. This experiment was repeated with improved results in the caligraphy of the spirit, who also signed his name.

The sitting was conducted in the usual gaslight of our house. The medium never touched the paper, and had nothing whatever to do with the experiment beyond holding the slate under the table with one hand, while the other rested on the table. The only sitters present were my wife and son and daughter.

The experiment, it will be noticed, was twice repeated, and on the second time with better success than on the first. The same words were written on each occasion. The paper was initialled and dated, and the slates were so tightly screwed together that the point of a knife could not be inserted between them. The Psychic was in his normal state throughout the experiment, and no muscular movements of any kind were noticeable, as he held the slate. Mr. Mould informs me, in answer to a letter of inquiry, that he "had subsequent experiments with the same Psychic, and obtained similar results, with the additional test of having the screw which locked the slates covered with gummed paper, affixed to the frame of the slate by a seal. . . . . The lad came alone to my house: he never touched the paper, nor even handled the slates until they were securely fastened." During every experiment there was "a full glare of light streaming from a three-globed chandelier, and a large fire." Mr. Mould adds that the persons present on each occasion were confined to his own family, and concludes, "I cannot be sure of anything transpiring around me if I must forswear the evidence of my senses on this occasion."

Mr. Mould is good enough to send me the paper for inspection. It contains the sketch of a profile, and three lines of writing. The latter is very tremulous, and was apparently written with difficulty. In one case a badly-formed letter has been afterwards corrected.

DICTATION BY THE EXPERIMENTER OF THE WORDS WRITTEN.

I HAVE already alluded, in giving my own personal testimony to one experiment in which I dictated the word which was found written within the slates. I draw attention to this as a noteworthy point in the evidence.

Mr. Alfred Russel Wallace, F.R.G.S., the eminent Naturalist, writes a letter to the *Spectator* of October 6, 1877, in which he records a similar case:—

SIR,—I trust you may consider the following experiment worthy of record in your paper, because it differs from cases of abnormal slate-writing, of which evidence was adduced at the trial of Slade, and because it affords a demonstration of the reality of the phenomenon, and the absence of imposture, from which there seems no escape. I confine myself to this one experiment, and narrate the essential facts only.

The sitting was at a private house in Richmond, on the 21st of last month. Two ladies and three gentlemen were present, besides myself and the medium, Dr. Monck. A shaded candle was in the room, giving light sufficient to see every object on the table round which we sat. Four small and common slates were on the table. Of these I chose two, and after carefully cleaning, and placing a small fragment of pencil between them, I tied them together with a strong cord, passed around them both lengthways and crosswise, so as effectually to prevent the slates from moving on each other. I then laid them flat on the table, without losing sight of them for an instant. Dr. Monck placed the fingers of both hands on them, while I and a lady sitting opposite me placed our hands on the corners of the slates. *From this position our hands were never moved, till I untied them to ascertain the result.* After waiting a minute or two, Dr. Monck asked me to name any short word I wished to be written on the slate. I named the word "God." He then asked me to say how I wished it written. I replied, "Lengthways of the slate;" then if I wished it written with a large or a small "g," and I chose a capital "G." In a very short time, writing was heard on the slate. The medium's hands were convulsively withdrawn, and I then myself untied the cord (which was a strong silk watch-guard lent by one of the visitors), and on opening the slates, found on the lower one the word I had asked for, written in the manner I had requested, the writing being somewhat faint and laboured, but perfectly legible. The slate, with the writing on it, is now in my possession.

The essential features of this experiment are—that I myself cleaned and tied up the slates; that I kept my hand on them all the time; that they never went out of my sight for a moment; and that I named the word to be written, and the manner of writing it after they were thus secured and held by me. I ask, how are these facts to be explained, and what interpretation is to be placed upon them?—I am, Sir, &c., ALFRED R. WALLACE.

I was present on this occasion, and certify that Mr. Wallace's account of what happened is correct.
EDWARD T. BENNETT.

Mr. Hensleigh Wedgwood, J.P., corroborates the fact from experience of his own with the same Psychic :—

Having engaged Dr. Monck to give me a sitting yesterday evening, I bought a couple of small slates, and tied them face to face with a fragment or two of slate pencil between them before Dr. Monk arrived. The slates were tied tightly together by a double fold of tape, the two ends of the knot being sealed to the framing to hinder the band from slipping. In addition to this, I sealed the edges of the slates together, so that they could not be separated from each other in the slightest degree without being broken. The slates were laid on the table, and in the course of the evening, in a fair light, Dr. Monck, under control, desired me to place them on my head, which I did accordingly, keeping hold of them with one hand. He asked me whether I would have the writing signed by my father or my grandfather. I told him, as they were both named Josiah, he might take his choice. He put one hand on the slates, and after a moment we all heard the scratching sound of pencil-writing upon them. As soon as this was done, I took the slates down and laid them on one side till the end of the séance. I then examined them by the full light of the gas, and satisfied myself that the seal on the edges of the slates were unbroken, and called the attention of the other sitters to this essential point. Having cut the tape I found the following message written lengthways on one of the slates, in a direction transverse to that of the tape-binding :—

> God bless you
> for ever.
> Josiah.

The Rev. Thomas Colley, late curate of Portsmouth, who has made a great number of experiments with Monck, has in his possession a pile of slates on which dictated messages have been written under conditions which preclude imposture.

Mr. Oxley, of Higher Broughton, near Manchester, records, on the 15th September, 1876, a case in which five sentences were written at the dictation of persons present. Each person wrote his name on a visiting card, and the five cards were then placed in the middle of the table, and covered with a handkerchief so as to secure the requisite darkness. A pencil was placed with the cards. Requested to say what he wished written on his card, each observer dictated a short sentence. When Mr. Oxley took the cards from under the handkerchief, these sentences were found written precisely as they had been dictated. The pencil was seen to move under the cover as if in the act of writing, while the Psychic was sitting motionless, in full view, eighteen inches from the pencil. Of the sentences so written, the first contained six words; the second, five; the third, three; the fourth, five, and the fifth, six.

On the next evening but one, another experiment was made, to show the rapidity with which these psychographs can be executed, and the experiment with the marked visiting cards was repeated.

On our being seated at the table, the gas was turned a little lower to modify the glare, but with quite sufficient light to let us see every object in the room distinctly. A good sized slate was lying on the table, and Dr. Monck (to whom I sat opposite) told me to take it up, clean it, show it to all assembled, and then to hold it under the table with my right hand. I did so, and, beginning to count, I had got to *nine*, when Dr. Monck said, "I think it is done." On bringing it up, I found one side and part of the other covered with writing, containing a message of eighty words. This most extraordinary experiment was accomplished in nine seconds, and certainly the medium did not touch the slate at all, for his hands were on the table, in full view, and he sat quite motionless. As soon as I put the slate under the table, I felt most distinctly the fingers of a hand gently touch my hand all over; it then took the slate from me for about half the time I was counting, and then returned it, again touching and stroking my hand.

My pencil was placed on the table, and we saw it begin to move: when it was raised, it floated in a horizontal position an inch above the table, and maintained that position while I counted thirty. The experiment of the writing on the marked card was repeated.

One of the sitters placed a slate under the table, the medium not touching it, and in about half a minute a message was written, containing thirteen lines, with seventy-five words. The medium then placed a small folding-slate on my head, touching it with his finger only for a moment. (I had cleaned the slate, and all saw there was nothing on it.) I counted three, and on opening the slate seventy-one words were written, in a beautifully neat hand. Again, on the following evening, seventy-one words were written in an extremely short space of time.

Dr. George Wyld contributes important evidence on this point. He has kindly put down for me an exact record of a crucial experiment, which I append in his own words. The bearing of this fact upon such allegations as those on the faith of which Slade was adjudged by the public to be an impostor is plain to see:—

I expected to be called as a witness in the second trial of Slade, and as Lankester's evidence was that "there was no time to produce the writing, and that therefore it had, in his case, been previously prepared," it seemed to me most important to be able to swear that writing could be produced by spirit-power with a rapidity beyond the capacity of *human* hands.

Accordingly I visited Slade, who readily consented to make a trial as I suggested.

We sat down to his usual table. Slade sat with his left hand resting on the table, and with his right hand he held an ordinary slate, on which was placed the customary bit of slate-pencil. This slate he passed steadily but rapidly below the corner of the flap of the table at his right hand. Each time he so passed it I examined the slate. He so passed it two or three times, without any result; but at last, after passing it as usual, on its emergence from below the flap of the table I found these words written in dusty slate-pencil writing, "Let this convince you."

I could not time Slade's actions while in progress, but subsequently I imitated his mode of passing the slate as closely as I possibly could, and my friends found that the operation occupied from three-quarters of a second to a second and a-half. I then timed the writing, and could find no one capable of writing the words in less than three seconds.

I considered at the time, and still consider, this experiment a complete refutation of Lankester's objection as to time. GEO. WYLD, M.D.

12 Great Cumberland Place, Hyde Park,
Dec. 30, 1877.

These facts receive a remarkable corroboration from two experiments recorded by Miss Kislingbury. The Psychic in this case was Watkins, above alluded to, and the experiments have a value which I shall hereafter note, which induces me to quote them *in extenso*, although I have before noticed the writing of the Russian word :—

Having read in *The Spiritualist* of October 12th, Mr. Epes Sargent's account of Mr. Watkins's slate-writing manifestations, and hearing at the same time that Mr. Watkins had arrived in New York, I took an early opportunity of visiting him, in company with my friend, Madame Blavatsky.

The medium began by asking us to write the names of three or four deceased friends on slips of paper, which he tore before our eyes from a fresh sheet of writing-paper. After writing the names, we folded the papers up tightly, at his request, and laid them in a little heap in front of us on the table. Mr. Watkins then stirred the pellets round with the point of a pencil, in order that we might not be able to distinguish one from the other. He requested me to take one in my hand, and to fix it on the point of his pencil; then holding it at arm's length, he said immediately, "This is the name of a sister of yours in the spirit-world, Clara Kislingbury, is that so?" Opening the pellet, I found the name to be correct; the statement that it was the name of my sister was equally so. The names on the three other pellets were rightly given, as well as the degree of relationship, including that of my maternal grandmother. I observed that Mr. Watkins had more difficulty in finding the name of one who was a friend, not connected with my family. He said at once, "This is the name of some one not a relation, I cannot see it so clearly;" but he finally succeeded in giving it correctly.

In the case of Madame Blavatsky, one of the names written by her was in Russian character, and the medium made several unsuccessful attempts to pronounce it, but at last declared it to be too "crack-jaw," and said he would try to get it written. He requested Madame Blavatsky to place her hand on a slate, under which he laid a small crumb of slate-pencil, in the manner of Slade. *Mr. Watkins did not hold the slate.* An instant after, on turning up the slate, the appellation, consisting of three names, was found written in full, and in Russian characters, with this curious exception, that one or two letters were exchanged for those of Latin character, having the same phonetic value; as, for instance, an *f*, pronounced in Russian *v*, but written *b*, was substituted for the latter. I will revert to this fact further on.

Mr. Watkins next took two small slates, and placing a point of pencil between them, held them firmly together at one end, while I held them at the other. The slate did not rest upon the table, but was held by us at arm's length, both standing. In a few moments one of the slates was covered on the inner side with writing signed "Alice Carey." The handwriting was not known to me, but was familiar to the medium, as frequently appearing in his experiments.

I use the word "experiments" advisedly, for two reasons. The first is, that Mr. Watkins did not "sit," except momentarily, during the whole hour that we were in his company, and then more often on the table than elsewhere. He walked nervously about the room, and occasionally fixed his eyes on us with a vacant look, especially when about to utter the desired name, or to describe something about the sitter. The second reason is, that Mr. Watkins does not habitually use the terms commonly accepted by Spiritualists, neither does he accept unreservedly the usual explanation of the phenomena, viz., that they are produced by the spirits of the departed, whose names are signed on the slate. He boldly *volunteered* the opinion that they are in many cases produced by the action of his own spirit, reading (independently of his will or knowledge) that which is latent in the mind of the sitter, or is immediately projected from it. He prefers to call the phenomenon "independent slate-writing," instead of "spirit-writing."

In the course of the experiments, Mr. Watkins said that in each instance, just before the writing began, he felt a sudden "drawing" from his whole body, and that he was unable to articulate distinctly; as soon as the writing was finished there was another jerk, and he felt himself again.

One more incident. Mr. Watkins told me to place my hand on a slate which was lying near me, and on which I had ascertained that there was nothing written. Mr. Watkins himself was at that moment lying back in a rocking-chair at a distance of *at least* eight feet from me, and talking to Madame Blavatsky. He ceased speaking for a moment, and then bidding me turn up the slate, I found it covered with writing, purporting to be a communication from my sister Clara, and signed with her name. The writing was quite unlike that signed "Alice Carey," but neither was it like mine or my sister's. The names of two other relatives which I had previously written on the pellets were mentioned, but *not those* of others equally dear to me, and of the same degree of relationship, and who were equally in my mind, *but were not written down*.

The above experiences are to my mind suggestive of a theory which will explain the discrepancies in the spelling of the Russian name. I leave the application to those whom it may concern, and who are more qualified than myself to form correct conclusions. Let it be borne in mind, however, that the medium himself avers that, except on rare occasions, and those special to himself—that is, when not sitting for the public—he has not only no evidence of the agency of departed spirits, but that there is no necessity for the hypothesis, nothing ever occurring which could not be performed by the action of his own spirit, working independently of his body, and seeking in the psychic emanations of those present the information (?) he is enabled to give them.

New York, October 26th, 1877.

The second experiment is recorded thus:—

The subject of will-power, and its probable influence on some spiritual manifestations, having been much discussed between Madame Blavatsky and myself, I determined to try an experiment in that direction. I went alone to Mr. Watkins, and I asked him to write some single word on a slate, and to turn the side of the slate so written on against the surface of the table, in order that it should not be seen by me. I in my turn did likewise. I then requested Mr. Watkins to hold with me my own double slate, between the folds of which I had placed a crumb of slate-pencil, and to will that his word should be written on it. I also willed that my word should be written. Mr. Watkins seemed rather incredulous over the business, and was genuinely surprised on opening the slates to find that the word I had willed should be written was upon the slate. "Let us try again," he said. "Very well," I replied; "but suppose we write something more this time, a sentence of three words." Mr. Watkins wrote, as appeared later on, the words, "*God is love.*" I wrote "*Love is eternal.*" Mr. Watkins took the folding slate with which we had before operated into his hands, saying: "I am impressed to hold the slate alone." Suddenly it struck me that he was stealing a march upon me, and I insisted on taking hold of the other end—first satisfying myself that nothing had been written. We heard the pencil at work, and on opening the slate found two sentences written: one was Mr. Watkins's, "*God is love;*" the other was *not* my sentence, but a third, "*Truth is mighty.*" I was immensely puzzled. "This is the effect neither of my will nor of yours, Mr. Watkins; whose is the third will that has been at work?" "I think I can tell you," he said; "while you were writing your sentence on the slate, I, having finished mine, began guessing what yours might be, and I thought 'Truth is mighty;' that is how I account for it." "I did not ask you to think, Mr. Watkins, but to will; however this is an interesting experiment, and goes still further to prove the theory I have in my mind. Now let us try another." But a sitter was announced, and I had no further opportunity of testing the strength of my own will-power against that of Mr. Watkins.

WRITING ANSWERS TO QUESTIONS WITHIN A BOX NAILED, TIED, AND SEALED UP.

THE evidence of Mrs. Andrews as to obtaining an answer to a question written by herself on the inner side of a slate, which was then screwed to another slate, will be remembered. As a test which, if it does not surpass, at least equals anything that has been recorded, I adduce the following case, recorded by Messrs. G. H. and W. P. Adshead with Monck. The case occurred thus.

Dr. R. S. Wyld, author of *The Physics and Philosophy of the Senses*, and other philosophical works, having been led to investigate Psychic phenomena, suggested certain tests which would appear to him satisfactory. Dwelling on the paramount necessity of obtaining the best procurable evidence for facts that so transcend ordinary experience, he suggested the following experiment :—" Let a box be properly taped, and the tapes knotted and sealed at each crossing. Let it contain a piece of writing-paper, with the signatures of the investigators thereon for identification, and a short piece of lead pencil. If a few words can be written on the paper whilst it is locked up, it is clear we have a proof which cannot be gainsayed."

Mr. W. P. Adshead accepted these conditions, and thus records the result of his experiment :—

In the afternoon of Friday, August 4th, I met Dr. Monck in Derby. I asked him if he had seen Dr. Wyld's letter. He said he had not. I described to him the test. "I have tried the experiment successfully several times," he replied. Dr. Monck was then controlled for two or three minutes by "Samuel," who said, in answer to my inquiry, that "if we would arrange for a séance in the evening he would do his best to repeat the experiment." We decided to do so, and met at the residence of Mrs. Ford. There were present Dr. Monck, Mrs. Ford, my brother, his wife, and myself.

In order that what occurred at the séance may be perfectly understood, it is necessary that I should here state that a day or two previously Dr. Monck received a letter from a gentleman in London, in which was enclosed a sealed packet, on the outside of which was written, "Not to be opened: nine questions to be submitted for answers." This packet Dr. Monck handed to my brother, asking him to keep it in his possession until answers to the questions could be formally requested.

A wooden box, with loose cover and string, were supplied by my brother; a sheet of note paper, envelope, pencil, wax, hammer and nails, together with two small hand-bells, were supplied by Mrs. Ford, so that not one of the articles which were to be used in the experiment about to be tried had previously been in the possession of Dr. Monck. The box was passed round for examination, and all agreed that it was most suitable for the purpose.

Dr. Monck then tore a piece from one corner of the sheet of note paper, and gave me the piece, which I put in my pocket. The paper was then passed round for inspection, and it was found to be blank, not having a mark of any kind upon it. We all saw Dr. Monck fold it up, and place it in the envelope, which he fastened up. The envelope was then initialed by each person present, and placed by me in the box with the two hand-bells and a pencil. In addition to cording and sealing, I had suggested that the lid of the box should be nailed down; this was accordingly done, each one driving in a nail, and all being quite satisfied that without any other fastening the contents were perfectly secure. However, in order to make assurance doubly sure, with a piece of cord that had not a break or knot in it, I tied the box, standing up to do so, in order to get greater purchase; in fact, so great was the strain on the cord, it could not be moved a quarter of an inch in any direction, and the edges of the box and lid were deeply indented by the operation. I tied the cord in several knots, leaving the ends about two inches long. The knots and the ends of the string I well covered with sealing wax, asking for a seal with which to impress it. As there was not one at hand, nothing remained but for two of the friends, acting on the suggestion of the moment, to remove the rings from their fingers, and with these I stamped the wax. This, I think, will dispose of the theory that the seals might be broken and re-sealed, to say nothing of the further difficulty involved, that of re-sealing without a light.

After sitting a short time in the light, sounds, as of the bells being moved, were heard to proceed from the box. We then saw it gently oscillate, and rise at one end about an inch from the table; then all was quiet. Nothing further occurring for some time, Dr. Monck—requesting us to place our hands upon the box, to assure ourselves it would not be interfered with in any way—asked us to put out the light, as it would increase the power. This was done, and in a few minutes "Samuel" took control of his medium. After a little conversation about the character of the séance, he was asked if he thought he could execute a piece of writing under the severe conditions which then obtained; he replied, "he thought he could," saying, "What shall I write?" My brother, remembering at the moment the sealed packet he had in his possession, said, "Be good enough to answer the questions contained in the sealed packet I have in my pocket."

Presently we heard the pencil at work, and in a very short time the task was accomplished. We were told to light up, and open the box. Before opening the box we examined it, and found the cord and the impressions of the rings on the wax perfect, and after cutting the cord, it was with great difficulty I could draw the nails and remove the lid. I took out the envelope, and found it to be the same I had placed there, as it bore the initials spoken of. I opened it, and took out the sheet of note paper, and immediately proceeded to fit in the piece torn from the corner, and which I had not parted with. The fit was perfect, for on the edges of the tear there were a projection and a corresponding indentation, which placed it beyond all dispute that the pieces belonged to each other. On one page of the note paper had been written with a pencil the following, with two or three other words, which, for obvious reasons, have been omitted :—

Aug. 4, 76. *Derby*.

Dear ——,

1. I think a change is probable; circumstances are often the policemen, peremptorily saying, "MOVE ON."
2. —— St. may be the one. Imitate me, and "please yourself."
3. If necessary we will impress you.
4. Town is the place for him.
5. No; lodge with a *stranger*.
6. Do I want you to burn your fingers? Haven't you had quite enough of *manufacturing*?
7. In neither department; but please yourself ——.
8. Don't leave London.
9. Yes; ask a few more questions; our advice is gratuitous.

SAMUEL, M. A. A., &c.

I now requested my brother to open the sealed packet, which he did in the presence of all. Inside was found a sheet of paper, on which was written the following in ink :—

My dear Spirit-Friends,—Feeling, as I do, the fact of your ability to advise your earth-friends, I ask your advice to the following questions to the best of your ability :—

No. 1. Do you think a change in my habitation is imminent?
2. Do you think the house in —— Street will be the one?
3. If not, can you impress me in which direction to go?
4. Do you think —— will remain in town?
5. If so, do you wish me to go with him to lodge?
6. Would you advise me to commence manufacturing again?
7. If so, in which department; in the —— or ——?
8. If either above, would you advise London or country?
9. If my spirit-friends have any further advice to offer, please do so on any subject concerning my welfare, as I wish to seek their guidance in all my steps.

The above questions are submitted by ——.

I think it will be conceded that the writing taken from the box supplied most appropriate answers to the questions on the paper taken from the sealed packet, but the problem to be solved is, how the answers came there. I have minutely detailed the facts as they occurred, and think the solution lies on the surface; but I will anticipate the possible suggestion, that by some means or other the medium had obtained a knowledge of the questions, and had previously written out the answers on a paper which he managed to introduce into the envelope after the sheet of note paper supplied by Mrs. Ford had been examined, and before the envelope was initialed, by observing that—in addition to the difficulty which such a suggestion must encounter in the fact that the piece of paper which I retained was torn from a blank sheet, and exactly fitted into the one on which the answers were written—there is the further difficulty of saying how, under the circumstances, any human being could have known what subject would be selected for the test-writing; for my brother solemnly affirms that not until after the box was securely fastened, and "Samuel" had asked what he should write about, did it occur to him to request that answers might be given to the questions enclosed in the packet which he had in his pocket. So that this portion of the phenomena, considered by Dr. Wyld decisive as to the truth of Spiritualism, was obtained under conditions even more severe than those he had suggested, for, in addition to being corded and sealed, the lid of the box was fastened down with nails.

Mr. G. H. Adshead had previously obtained a similar success :—

Dr. Wyld, of Aberdeenshire, recently proposed the following test as "a final and absolute proof of Spiritualism, which the most illustrious opponent would be unable to gainsay." As soon as we suggested it to Dr. Monck, he agreed to try it. Nine of us placed our signatures on a sheet of paper (supplied by myself, and never before seen by the Doctor), which each one had previously examined on both sides, in the full blaze of two gas jets, and found to be blank. A non-Spiritualist—an entire stranger to the Doctor—folded the paper and dropped it into the box, together with my pencil. Another non-Spiritualist fastened the lid with four nails, which he drove in with a hammer to their heads. With a piece of strong white tape—supplied by Mrs. Ford—he then tied the box round all its sides, made several knots at each crossing of the tape, and fastened the ends to the top of the box with sealing-wax, on which a non-Spiritualist's lettered seal was pressed. Until the box was thus secured, Dr. Monck purposely sat back from the table, and did not even touch or put a finger near the box, paper, tape, &c. In a few minutes "Samuel" controlled the medium, and asked me if I wished him to write anything special on the imprisoned paper. I said, "Yes; write 'My love to Louie.'" He replied, "It shall be done in the twinkling of an eye," and in the same breath said, "Open the box." Mr. W. Smith, of Gerard Street, who had fastened the lid down, now carefully cut the tape, to which the seal still adhered without flaw, and by the aid of a screw-driver, with considerable difficulty succeeded in opening the box, and (two gas jets being at the full immediately above it) we all saw the paper taken out by Mr. Smith, and found it to be the original sheet, containing all our signatures, and the whole of the rest of what had been blank space on both sides of the sheet was covered with large and very legible writing in "Samuel's" well-known hand. On one side was written, "All hail! Present my compliments to Dr. Wyld, and ask him whether this is what he wants. I have often done this and far greater things through this medium.—SAMUEL." On the other side was, "Aug. 6, 1876.—My love to Louie." A detailed statement of these facts was carefully drawn up on the spot at once, and signed, for publication, by all the witnesses whose signatures had been placed on the test-paper before the experiment.

To anything short of a superfine hyper-criticism, which will accept nothing except personal evidence—and not that, in many cases—I cannot see how such testimony as this can be set aside. The conditions under which the experiment was made are conclusive. It is, indeed, only fair to say, that the phenomena which I have witnessed in the presence of this particular Pyschic, are produced under conditions extremely satisfactory, and most favourable for exact observation. This has been so in a great number of recorded cases, as in the following which I append as a specimen of the care taken in testifying to these facts. It is written and signed by Joseph Clapham, of Keighley, under date Oct. 6, 1876, and records the conditions under which Monck placed himself there.

There is absolutely no room for deception, because—
1. A stranger to the Doctor, who is a well-known sceptic, thoroughly cleans the slate.
2. While this person holds it, all in the circle inspect it, and pronounce it to be free from writing.
3. The sceptic holds it under the table, at least four feet from the medium.
4. Instantly he *feels*, as well as hears, the pencil writing on the slate.
5. All the sitters hear the same sound.
6. No person in the flesh, except the before-mentioned "sceptic," touches the slate from the moment the latter cleans it till he holds it up to the light that all may see it is full of writing.
7. Dr. Monck's hands are on the table in full view, and perfectly still the whole time.
8. The whole of the sitting is in a good clear light.
9. We sit in a room belonging to one of us, which we enter and search some time before the Doctor arrives.
10. I must not omit to add that the Doctor has permitted me to thoroughly search his clothes, both immediately before and after the sitting.
11. And, finally, the communication on the slate has sometimes been a direct reference to what we have been singing.

Finally, I adduce here a curious result obtained by Mr. Coleman on glass. The material used apparently makes no difference. In this case, as in many others, the writing was done by a material hand.

Of this class of manifestation I have had, from time to time, many, but nothing I think worth your notice, except it may be messages received by me in 1869, written on *glass*, of which I have preserved two specimens. I don't remember that I ever published a record of these writings, and I may as well describe them. I prepared pieces of thick plate glass, and covered the upper surface with a light coating of white paint. The medium took hold of one end, and I of the other, and we held it immediately beneath the table, the gas burning brightly over our heads. In an instant, I felt something like a hand using, as it appeared, the finger-nail to write the message. I had been talking with the presumed spirit of a young girl known to me, who had given her name, and my questions were answered on the prepared glass. She said, " I am in heaven ;" and I asked, " Where is your heaven ?" and the reply—which I have preserved, all the others being rubbed out—was, " I bring my heaven with me.—ISABELLA." And, as I intended to keep the glass, I placed it again beneath the table, and asked the spirit to add the date, when 1869 was added. I may as well say, that the writing was quite unlike Isabella's, and gave no evidence of identity, but of the fact of an intelligent entity having written upon the glass, there can be no doubt whatever."

CORRESPONDENCE IN "THE TIMES."

BEFORE I summarise the evidence which has been brought forward, I may be permitted to refer in passing to such points of testimony as were brought out in the correspondence in *The Times*, at the time of the Slade prosecution. Into the vexed questions raised during that period, it is not my purpose to enter. I have no desire to stir up the embers of old fires; nor do I wish to assume a controversial attitude in presenting my evidence. It would be easy for me to impeach the conduct of that memorable prosecution, and to show how much reason we, who have dived somewhat further below the surface than the prosecutors had, have to find fault with the measure of justice served out to us. At another time I shall be ready to do this, even more fully than I have already done it:* for the present, it is outside my line of argument, and would impede my purpose. I have no desire to impugn the action of those gentlemen who have thought it their duty to prosecute Slade. Nor have I any intention of questioning their beliefs. My object is historical, not controversial. My business is simply to place on record facts which, I hope, may lead a discerning public to agree with me in the opinion, that the conclusion they arrived at was hasty, and

---

* The Slade Case. By M. A., Oxon.

that the method of investigation employed was not the scientific method. I do not set myself to impugn, or even to influence the beliefs of any man. I only desire to record certain facts, which I invite him to square with those beliefs. If he can disprove my facts, I shall be happy to listen to his argument. If he can accept them, and fit them in to his mind, I shall be happy to recognise a friend in thought. But if he can do neither, and if he still tries to shun my facts— if he falls back on *à priori* impossibilities, or shifts from one leg to another, in the vain hope of avoiding them by procrastination, halting between two opinions, nearly as uncomfortable in the one as in the other—I can but take off my hat to his logic, and pity his dilemma.

During the agitation that succeeded Professor Lankester's assault upon the slate, several letters found a place in *The Times*. It is not worth while to quote the correspondence, and I may record here, as strengthening my argument, the experience of a man who is perfectly familiar with these facts, and is, so far, a better judge than one who is not.

Mr. Joy, M. Inst. C.E., late of the R.A., writes from the Junior United Service Club thus :—

1. Slade sat on my left, facing me, and in such a position that not only his legs and his feet, but his whole body, as well as both hands and arms, were in full view during the whole séance, except when he was avowedly holding the slate under the table, when one hand and fore-arm were concealed.
2. The writing always came on the upper side of the slate.
3. On one occasion I wrote a question on one side of the

slate, holding it in such a position that Slade could not possibly see what I was writing, not that it would have made any difference if he had done so; for, after I had turned the slate so as to have the writing downwards, Slade took hold of one corner, while I still held the other, and, while both were thus holding it, we passed it underneath the table, when Slade immediately let go, and placed both his hands on the top of the table. Under these circumstances I got a distinct answer to my question written on the upper side of the slate.

Mr. G. C. Joad adds his testimony:—

I took with me a book-slate—*i.e.* two slates joined down one side so as to close like a book. I first examined Dr. Slade's fingers; the nails were cut down so low that I do not believe he could have picked up a pin, and there was no mark of a piece of pencil having been pushed between the nail and the flesh. I then inspected Dr. Slade's slate, which was on the table, and initialed one corner; it was then immediately placed close against the under side of the table at the corner, in such a position that I could see Dr. Slade's thumb on the rim of the slate projecting beyond the edge of the table nearest to him, while the corner of the slate with my initials was just visible beyond the side of the table nearest to me. A scratching was at once heard, and on removal a message was seen written on the upper side where my initials were. I need hardly say I kept my eyes on the visible portion of the slate all the time.

I then produced my own slate, perfectly clean, a tiny piece of pencil was placed between the flaps, the slate was closed, and at once placed beneath the table. I could see by one end that it was kept closed; a message was written inside, the writing was left, and the piece of pencil placed on the inner surface that remained clean. This time Dr. Slade, on the slate being closed, raised it, and rested one corner on the point of my left shoulder, the slate projecting to the front, so that by turning my head I could see the whole of it. It was moved directly from the table to my shoulder, and I did not lose sight of it for a second. A scratching began, and on the three taps being heard, the slate was placed on the table and opened, when on the previously clean surface was seen written, "Cannot do more; let this be proof.—Allie." Perhaps I may as well mention that no raps or kicks occurred to distract my attention.

GEORGE C. JOAD.

Oakfield, Wimbledon Park, W., Sept. 18th.

And Professor Barrett, F.R.C.S., writes a very commendable letter, in which, protesting against the brute-force argument of Mr. Lankester, he details what he himself obtained—drawing attention to what may throw much light upon obscure phenomena of this kind—viz., the mental phenomena of transfusion of thought, and generally of the action of one mind upon another, across space, without the intervention of the senses.

Soon after my first sitting with Slade I noticed the same suspicious circumstances to which Professor Lankester alludes—namely, the movement of the tendons of the wrist, the coughing, fidgeting, &c., and, in addition, the fact of Slade always sitting back to the light and sideways, so that the front of his person is in comparative shade, though generally in full view. Naturally the first explanation that suggested itself was one something like that given by Professor Lankester, but observations on several subsequent sittings to test this and other theories failed, in my opinion, to establish any one of them so conclusively as Professor Lankester asserts.

Instead of forcibly interrupting Slade and discovering writing when none was supposed to be present—which is the substance of Professor Lankester's exposure, and to which Slade might furnish a ready reply, based upon his ignorance of when the writing does actually occur—I made the following experiment :—

Taking a slate clean on both sides, I placed it on the table so that it rested above, although its surface could not touch a fragment of slate pencil. In this position I held the slate firmly down with my elbow; one of Slade's hands was then grasped by mine, and the tips of the fingers of his other hand barely touched the slate. While closely watching both of Slade's hands, which did not move perceptibly, I was much astonished to hear scratching going on apparently on the under side of the table, and when the slate was lifted up I found the side facing the table covered with writing. A similar result was obtained on other days; further, an eminent scientific friend obtained writing on a clean slate when it was held entirely in his own hand, both of Slade's being on the table.

This seems to be the place to add the testimony of one who has had the combined advantages of vast opportunity for observation, and of a training in exact scientific methods which fits him to utilise the opportunities placed in his way.

Mr. W. H. Harrison, Editor of *The Spiritualist*, writes to me :—

Before Dr. Slade came to London, years of observation at numerous séances had proved to me that the materialised hands common at séances were most frequently the duplicates of those of the medium, and produced nearly the same handwriting. The first messages I saw produced in the presence of Dr. Slade were given in broad daylight, under such clear test physical conditions as to leave no room for the imposture theory in the mind of any trained or competent scientific observer. I noticed that they were nearly always in the handwriting of the medium; and this, which to an ignorant person would have been indicative of imposture, was in favour of the genuineness of the phenomena to an expert. On leaving the room after the séance I had a short talk with Mr. Simmons, and without telling him what I knew, but merely to test his integrity, I asked him whether the handwriting on the slates bore any resemblance to that of Dr. Slade. Without hesitation, he replied that there was usually a strong resemblance. This shows the truthfulness and absence of exaggeration incidental to the statements of Mr. Simmons, who is one of the coolest and quietest men living; had he been prone to making statements in advance of the facts, he would have tried to make the phenomena more wonderful, and have said that there was generally no resemblance between the handwritings. But the truth was thus unreservedly told by Mr. Simmons directly after he reached London, and was forthwith printed by me in *The Spiritualist*, for the information of observers at Dr. Slade's séances.

In dealing with such facts, the testimony of skilled observers is of most value. A reputed scientific man, ignorant of astronomy, who entered an observatory and said that he knew more about the work done there than astronomical experts, and who behaved with "bounce" generally, would not be recognised by the scientific world as a creditable representative.

SUMMARY OF FACTS.

The sum of what I have stated may be resolved into the following propositions :—

1. That there exists a Force which operates through a special type of human organisation, and which is conveniently called PSYCHIC FORCE.
2. That this force is (in certain cases) demonstrably governed by Intelligence.
3. That this Intelligence is (in certain cases) provably not that of the person or persons through whom the Force is evolved.
4. That this Force, thus governed by an external Intelligence, manifests its action in (amongst other methods) the writing of coherent sentences without the intervention of any of the usual methods of writing. Such abnormal writing is conveniently called Psychography.
5. That the evidence for the existence of this Force, thus governed by an external Intelligence, rests upon :
    (a) The evidence of the observer's senses.
    (b) The fact that a language other than that known to the Psychic is frequently used.
    (c) The fact that the subject-matter of the writing is frequently beyond the knowledge of the Psychic.

(*d*) The fact that it is demonstrably impossible to produce the results by fraud under conditions similar to those under which the phenomena are obtained.

(*e*) The fact that these special phenomena are produced not only in public, and for gain, but in private, and without the presence of any person outside of the family circle.

DEDUCTIONS, EXPLANATIONS, AND THEORIES.

I HAVE now brought forward such facts as I consider necessary out of the large number at my disposal. If I have not quoted some on which, because they come within their own personal experience, some of my friends may rely, I must remind them that my object is not to write an exhaustive chronicle, but only to bring forward such cases as will explain and enforce my argument. I cannot quote all, and I have used an editor's discretion in selecting.

I desire now, in concluding my argument, to draw attention to some points which will throw light on the theories which have been maintained.

Dr. Carter Blake has recorded his opinion that the Force, whose action he observed with Slade, " acted from a spot or spots separate from " him. By this he does not, of course, imply that the Psychic is not the medium through whom the Force is evolved. Plainly he is. Those who have had opportunity of holding the hands of a Psychic during the time when he is passing into the state during which phenomena occur, are familiar with the pulsations and throbs which evidence the surging of the force within him. Convulsive shudders agitate his frame, and these are frequently communicated to the observer, even though he be not a Psychic himself.

I have good cause to remember one of my first experiments with two powerful Psychics, Herne and Williams. After three unsuccessful experiments, the fourth resulted in such a convulsive action of my right arm as to force my hand to beat the table with the most surprising vehemence. I was perfectly powerless to control my arm, and the result was that my hand was so bruised as to be comparatively useless, and very positively painful, for some days afterwards. It was only the arm that was affected. In all other respects I was in a perfectly normal state.

Dr. C. Blake notes a similar fact in recording one of his experiments with Slade. "His hands being on both mine in the centre of the table, the muscles of my fore-arms were seized with a convulsive motion, and the waves of this motion, according to my impression, proceeded from my elbows to the finger-tips, and not the converse, as some people might be led to expect. The sensation was unlike what would have been produced by an electric battery under the table, and was more like what I should imagine was the sensation of the *aura epileptica*." This convulsive movement is gradually communicated to the table, if the Psychic's hands are placed upon it. I have frequently noticed a distinct rhythmical pulsation in the table, commencing some time before any other objective manifestation of the Force is shown, and gradually increasing until it culminates in percussive sounds, or in movements of the table. When this condition is

Deductions, Explanations, and Theories. 131

obtained, it is frequently unnecessary for the Psychic, or, indeed, for any one, to touch the table any more. The movements will continue at request, without the contact of any hands, until the stored-up Force is exhausted, when contact again becomes necessary.

In Slade's case, the making and breaking of the contact of hands, and consequent cessation and recommencement of the writing was very suggestive. I have alluded to this point before, and several of the records which I have quoted make mention of it. The subjoined account, written by Mr. Conrad W. Cooke, of the Society of Telegraph Engineers, puts it clearly:—

On the afternoon of Saturday, August 19th, 1876, I, in company with Professor ——, had a "sitting" with Dr. Slade, at a house in Upper Bedford Place, Russell Square. We arrived at the house a little before three o'clock, and as Dr. Slade was giving a seance to some other gentlemen, we were asked into a front drawing-room on the first floor.

Presently two gentlemen came out of the inner room, handed a fee to the secretary, and went away. Dr. Slade then came in, and took us into the adjoining room, which was an ordinary back drawing-room of such houses, furnished as lodging-houses generally are, and having a rectangular double-flap table in the middle of the room, rather farther from the window than the centre of the room would be. This table was covered with a somewhat shabby coloured table-cover, which Dr. Slade removed. He then asked us to examine the table. This we did by moving it, turning it up, and trying it by tapping it in various places. As far as we could see, it was a perfectly ordinary table; the flaps were of the ordinary thickness, and to all appearance quite solid.

The table-cover was not replaced, and we, at Dr. Slade's request, sat at the table in the following manner:—Dr. Slade sat with his back to the window and facing the wall which divided us from the room in which he had previously been waiting. I sat opposite to and facing him, and therefore having the window in front of me; Professor ——— sat between us, and at right angles to the way we were sitting, having Dr. Slade to his left and myself to his right.

The room was in no way darkened, and the day, though generally cloudy, was interspersed with gleams of sunshine. I mention this to show that what we saw was in broad open daylight, in a room illuminated by a large window facing towards the west.

We sat, as I have said, at three sides of the table, with our hands upon it, and touching one another, forming what Dr. Slade called a "chain." Professor ———'s left hand rested on the back of the right hand of Dr. Slade, Dr. Slade's left hand was upon my right, and my left upon Professor ———'s right.

In this way we sat for perhaps three or four minutes, when the table gave two or three distinct tremendous pulsations, at first feeble and far between, but following closer upon one another, and becoming more decided in a few minutes. These were followed by gentle taps such as would be produced by a finger-nail tapping on the table, and then by raps becoming louder until they violently shook the latter and almost lifted it momentarily from the ground.

Dr. Slade then said, "Are you here, Allie?" Taps came on the table as if in reply, and Dr. Slade produced an ordinary school-slate, and biting off a piece from the end of a slate-pencil, he placed a piece about the size of a rice-grain on the slate, which he held under the table, pressing it up against the under side of the flap, which was over Professor ———'s knees. During this time the "chain" was maintained as before, except that Dr. Slade had but one hand joining ours, the other being employed to hold the slate. In holding the slate under the table, he did so by clasping the edge of the table and the slate together, after the manner of a clamp, so that his thumb was above the table. Immediately the slate was held against the table, we distinctly heard a slate-pencil writing on it, and when it ceased Dr. Slade pulled the slate away, apparently as if he encountered resistance, sliding it away from the edge in a manner very similar to sliding away an armature from a tolerably powerful permanent magnet, and upon the slate there were words written in a very clear hand.

Professor —— then asked Dr. Slade if he thought writing could be produced on the slate if it were *above* the table. Dr. Slade asked the question verbally, and placing the slate, as before, under the flap, the following words were written on it, " I do not know, but I will try." The " grain " of slate pencil was then placed on the table and covered by the slate, upon which Dr. Slade placed the palm of his left hand, his other hand being above the table and touching ours. The sound of the writing immediately commenced, and continued for several minutes, only stopping whenever any of us lifted a hand so as to " break the chain," as Dr. Slade expressed it. When the slate was turned up, it was perfectly covered with small, clear writing, a sort of essay upon the beneficial and harmless nature of Spiritualism, which it called by that name, and finishing up with the signature "*A. F. Slade.*"

Professor —— then requested to be allowed to hold the slate himself. A grain of slate-pencil was placed on the slate, which he held under the flap of the table, and pressing it up against it. In a moment the writing commenced, and a word or two was written on the slate. During the experiment both Dr. Slade's hands were above the table. A few minutes after, when the slate was held under the table, the following words were written:—" Good-bye, I cannot do any more," and after that no more writing or raps were produced, and we came away.

In the above notes I have simply stated the facts as they took place before my eyes and those of my friend in open daylight, on an afternoon in August, between three and four o'clock, and I offer no comments as to their cause.

Several observers noticed the fact that Slade's hands, when in contact with their own, were feverishly hot, and emitted a crackling, detonating sound. He would withdraw them as though the contact burnt him. I specially noticed this during the writing while I held the slate. After Slade had made a few downward passes over my arm, my fingers tingled, and I heard distinct detonating noises in the table.

These detonations sometimes are so powerful as to split the slate to fragments. Mr. Wedgwood's double-hinged slate was thus broken into minute pieces. The Rev. J. Page Hopps took away with him a slate which, in an unaccountable manner, *on his way home* was similarly pulverised. Several other observers have recorded the same action of what is apparently an explosive force within the object—not something that acts on it from without. And the Rev. Thomas Colley, writing on December 14, 1877, gives a very instructive record of a similar kind. A gentleman had forwarded to Monck a slate which he had so prepared as to render it impossible that it should be tampered with. He had embedded over the slate a plate of stout glass by means of plaster of Paris, leaving a space of about an inch between the slate and the glass. Into this chamber a fragment of pencil was introduced. The slate was perfectly clean, and it was physically impossible to write upon its inner surface by any normal means. Mr. and Mrs. Colley, together with Mr. and Mrs. Cranstoun, of the Tyrol, met Monck on the 14th December, and then and there the word desired by the gentleman who devised the test was clearly written. That word was *Tangier*. It was, in an unlucky moment for the safety of that slate, proposed that an attempt should be made to add a word at the separate dictation of each person present. The glazed slate, probably to obtain the necessary darkness, was placed under the table, and

Deductions, Explanations, and Theories.   135

the two gentlemen had each a foot upon it. Mr. Colley describes a sensation of throbbing within the slate—a heaving as when the confined steam lifts the lid of a kettle—and in a moment an explosion took place that scattered it in fragments over the carpet, *like spray from a fountain.* Mr. Colley instantly took up the slate, and found the words written in the order in which they had been dictated.

The interesting part of this narrative, apart from the crucial test contained in it, is the explosive action of the force, and the sensation of throbbing which Mr. Colley, by the accident of having his foot on the brick, was enabled to feel before the explosion took place. It would seem as if the little chamber between the glass and slate were made a receptacle in which the force conveyed through the Psychic was stored, just as, I believe, the table is charged with the force before any manifestation is given of its presence.

So much we are able to gather as to the source and operation of this Psychic Force. It is the "mesmeric fluid" of Mesmer; the odyle of Reichenbach; the nerve-aura of other investigators.

When we come to consider the method of its direction, we are on more precarious ground. So many theories have been propounded that their bare enumeration will suffice to show the lines on which speculation has worked.

Dr. Collyer is a type of those who consider that the phenomenon of Psychography is due to the unconscious action of the will of the Psychic. I append an interesting statement of his views, extracted from a pamphlet published by him at the time of the Slade prosecution. His views are not original, but the extract which I quote gives a convenient exposition of them :—

I will briefly narrate my experience with Mr. Henry Slade, and will confine my remarks to the automatic writing, leaving the various other phenomena for another occasion to describe. On the 6th day of October, 1876, at 7 p.m., I called at 8 Upper Bedford Place. I was shown into the drawing-room, where I found Mr. Henry Slade, Mr. Simmons, and two young ladies. After some few minutes, Mr. Slade and myself went into a small back room. There were two gaslights turned on to their full extent, making the room as light as gas could make it.

Mr. Slade took hold of my hands, and after a few moments he was in "the state." This transition was accompanied by the usual nervous twitchings. He told me to clean the slate which lay on the table. I did so, both with a sponge and then with my handkerchief. I never let go of the said slate, which he placed under the corner of the table. A small piece of slate pencil was placed on the upper surface of the slate. In less than ten seconds the said slate was written on, and in ten seconds more eight lines of writing, filling up the entire upper surface of the slate, were written.

As I have before stated, Mr. Slade believes that this was written by his wife's spirit. What he believes is quite beside the fact of writing occurring under circumstances that none of your wiseacres and tricksters could imitate. It was Slade's blind faith that the writing was spiritually produced, that enabled his Will-power to embody the thought. Having attended the trial at the Bow Street police court, I heard the childish propositions of chemical pencils, sympathetic inks, and so forth. I, accordingly, to meet all such objections, purchased of a stationer in Holborn two white porcelain slates, 7 inches long, 5 broad; these I took with me to Slade's rooms on Friday, Nov. 2nd, at noon. We retired into the same room as on the previous occasion. Mr. Slade sat for twenty minutes, but entirely failed, and said he had no power. I was not in the least astonished, as I have known persons for weeks to lose all power. On the following Sunday, Nov. 5, at noon, I again visited Mr. Slade. I untied the slates myself, broke off a piece of Cumberland lead, one-eighth of an inch in length, which I placed between the slates, and retied them together with the tape I had brought with me. The slates were then placed on the top of the table, Mr. Slade's fingers being in contact with the frame of the upper slate, his other hand was on my own. I distinctly heard the writing going on or being made. On opening the slates these words were written:—

"We cannot write with this point of pencil.—A. W. SLADE."

I retied the slate, leaving within the original piece of pencil.

An ordinary slate, which I carefully cleaned, was placed on the top of the table; on the under surface of the slate I heard the writing taking place. I had my elbow on the slate all the time. On turning the slate I found forty-nine words, written in less than three minutes by my watch. On returning to the drawing-room, I found a gentleman who had brought a folding-slate with him; this was written on both sides—that is, the upper and lower surface, inside the folded part of the slate. There were sixty-four words. At page 94 of my work, *Exalted States of the Nervous System* (Renshaw, 356 Strand), I use these words: "Faith and Will,—The power of the will, in the ordinary normal state, is confined to the immediate acts essential to the functions of life; but it may be educated (during an abnormal state) so as to be directed out of or beyond the ordinary channel, so that brain phenomena, or abnormal states, may be induced at the will of the individual. In order to arrive at perfect control of the organs not normally under the influence of the will, much time is required."

At page 106 I state: "The embodiment of thought is the cerebral representation or production of the figure thought of. If there be sufficient nervo-vital fluid at the command of the medium, he is enabled to project an embodiment which will, for the time being, under the direction of the will-power, manifest all the conditions of an independent existence."

The medium must necessarily be an extremely sensitive person—even morbidly so. How, then, is it possible that he can be calm and self-possessed, exercise mental concentration or will-power, if he is purposely rendered irritable; his sensitiveness wounded by wanton, puerile opposition? It cannot be expected that if the necessary conditions to success are destroyed that successful results can follow. It would be as unphilosophical to break your watch, and then to grumble because it ceased to keep time.

No man is a greater admirer of pure philosophy and close inductive reasoning than myself. I also abhor with detestation and contempt those upstart parvenus in science who imagine that by *coups de main* they can solve the most recondite revelations of brain function. It cannot be forgotten that the College of Physicians of London ignored both Harvey and Jenner. It should not be forgotten that the Royal Society of Great Britain received the report of Benjamin Franklin's experiments, showing the identity of lightning with other electrical phenomena, with a shout of laughter.

Napoleon referred the subject of steam navigation to the Academy of Science. The result was that the Academy pronounced the idea to be "a ridiculous notion." When George Stephenson first proposed railroad travelling, how was the idea treated by the British House of Commons? Did not his distinguished son, Robert Stephenson, with all England, ridicule the French project of digging a canal at Suez? Still, the British nation a few years subsequently gave four millions sterling for an interest in the same canal! Who, fifty years since, would not have been pronounced a madman if he had had the temerity to state the practicability of holding in a few minutes communication with his friends in Australia? Cases could be multiplied showing the ignorance of the most intellectual in matters which are beyond their knowledge. The universe abounds in mysteries, exciting only the barren wonder of the desponding observer, but stimulating the philosophical to untiring and earnest research. To contradict past experience is a certain indication of error; to march beyond it is the truest indication of genuine discovery. If ignorance is punishable with three months' hard labour, who could escape the amusing task of continually walking upstairs?

Slade is not responsible for his want of knowledge as to the *modus operandi* of the most recondite phenomena connected with cerebral function. All he knows is, that these phenomena do not occur under certain conditions. It is not because he verily believes that they are produced by the spirit of his late wife, that such a belief comes within the sphere of criminal jurisdiction. I am not responsible for Slade's ideas. I am thoroughly convinced he is honest in his belief. What concerns myself is the production of these cerebral phenomena. My conviction of the fact that they are produced without the least attempt at trickery or fraud, is a conviction arrived at after thirty-five years' investigation. That many persons with partially-developed powers have resorted to deception I am equally convinced. I have discovered on many occasions false representations, but these do not militate against the genuine phenomena. There is scarcely a subject with which the human mind is conversant that may not be simulated or imitated so closely as to deceive and betray the unsuspecting.

I am as satisfied of the genuineness of the automatic writing presented by Henry Slade, of the United States, as I am of my own existence, or that the sun gives light, or is the cause of light, or of any other physical phenomenon, universally admitted. I do not find fault with the learned magistrate who defined "palmistry" to be analogous to these new recondite mental phenomena. Nor do I blame Mr. Henry Slade for believing that the phenomena are produced by his deceased wife's spirit. I am firmly convinced that if he had not this belief the phenomena would not be produced. Blind faith is essential to the exercise of will-power.

It is the will-power during an abnormal or exalted state of brain which produces all these varied phenomena, no matter how diversified or apparently complicated.

Absolute blind faith (not exercisable during the normal state of existence) is necessary to the full development of will-power. Doubt your own capacity, and it ceases to exist. Conviction of power is the surest road to success; "he who hesitates is lost." It is really ridiculously funny to find men of the most ordinary mental faculties writing of the "Common Course of Nature."

All the world believed the postulates advanced by Aristotle, and these were defined as "The Laws of Nature" until Galileo and Newton demonstrated the contrary. As to the laws of falling bodies and gravitation, for two thousand years the whole world had spoken of the "Common Course of Nature." Common enough would poor Nature be if interpreted by such conjuring mechanicians. What is that which we entitle a Law of Nature? Is it, as is generally conceived, an abstract sovereign rule of Divine authority before the beginning of the world's existence? Or is it only a synthetical epitome of Nature's operations, such as human experience and assiduity has found out, and human ingenuity arranged? Here, on this very topic, is an error most prevalent, even amongst the men best versed in science. They are too apt to confound scientific theory, conventionally stamped, as a "law of Nature," as an original principle established by the fiat of Omnipotence. The poor wretch who has the temerity or foolish hardihood to question its validity is denounced as a heretic to the order of Nature herself. Roger Bacon was excommunicated by the Pope for such a crime, and imprisoned ten years, accused of having dealings with the devil. At that period (the 13th century) professors were bound, under oath, to follow no other guide than Aristotle. "There is a wide difference between the idols of the human mind and ideas of the Divine mind."

Dr. Geo. Wyld entertains a somewhat similar idea. In an elaborate paper printed in the *Spiritualist* of Dec. 14, 1877, he maintains the opinion "that all the phenomena we have yet obtained *might* be produced by the spirits of the living." Respecting Slade's Psychography, he "believes that it was produced by his own partially entranced spirit," although Slade was, *to all appearance, in his normal state at the time.*

This theory finds a curious illustration in the experiments recorded by Miss Kislingbury, which I have already quoted. There, however, the Psychic's will was decidedly not the only active cause. And, most probably, this may be so in any given case. Dr. Collyer's idea is that most in accordance with the ancient belief. Those who in days of old have studied the mysteries of occult phenomena have left for us a more or less bewildering record of their conclusions. Those who are curious enough to desire to peep behind the veil, and to master what the wisdom of the ancients has collected, may do so by perusing a work which has recently been published by Bouton of New York—ISIS UNVEILED: *a Master-Key to the Mysteries of Ancient and Modern Science and Theology.* By H. P. Blavatsky. There he will find, scattered up and down through two huge volumes—master-pieces of industry and erudition—much that will attract his attention and exercise his thought. And there, too, he will find the views of the ancients and mediævalists respecting the innate power of the human spirit set forth at length.

They believed that the human spirit, properly trained to energize through its will, had incalculable powers; that its action was by no means limited to the body in which it was imprisoned, but extended, under favouring circumstances, to almost any distance. They held that this phenomenon of Psychography, with which they were perfectly familiar, was effected by the spirit of the Psychic just as really as when his hand held the pencil and framed the letters.

They would say that such performances as we are familiar with are but the unconscious and feeble products of an untrained spirit, which possesses magical powers without knowing it. These unconscious and unregulated Psychic phenomena they would discourage, and would substitute for their feeble and uncertain results the sure and calculated efforts of a trained Will. Man, they say, an Incarnate Spirit, has in himself all he needs for the production of the most apparently miraculous results. He is lord of creation, with the "promise and potency" within him of all, even creative power, did he only know it.

The Kabalist is very strong in his claims, but he is at least coherent. Both Dr. Wyld and Dr. Collyer would seem to mix up two totally different states: one which I call Psychism, in which the Psychic is so far from exercising the power of his will with that concentrated energy which alone avails, that he must *ex hypothesi* be passive and at perfect rest in order to obtain results; and another, which is the state of conscious and concentrated Will-power—a state as positive as the other is negative—one that admits of no passivity, but is characterized by severest energy.

There are, indeed, grades of distinction between all three explanations; and the curious reader may amuse himself, without experiencing much fear of failure, by suggesting difficulties which neither of the modern theorists can hope to solve.

In Dr. Morin's *Journal de Magnetisme*, published in Paris, at a time when table-turning was at its height, a letter was printed which contains statements of opinion bearing upon what I am now saying. I quote from the same work of Madame Blavatsky's before alluded to:—

We, who well know the value of the phenomenon, . . . are perfectly sure that after having charged the table with our magnetic *efflux*, we have called to life, or created, an intelligence analogous to our own, which, like ourselves, is endowed with a free will—can talk and discuss with us with a degree of superior lucidity, considering that the resultant is stronger than the individual, or rather the whole is larger than a part of it. . . . The phenomenon is as old as the world. . . . The priests of India and China practised before the Egyptians and the Greeks. The savages and the Esquimaux know it well. It is the phenomenon of Faith, sole source of every prodigy.

This is the magic secret of the Kabalist, the grand truth enunciated in days long past by Jesus Christ —"Thy faith hath saved thee," "If ye have faith as a grain of mustard seed, ye shall say to this mountain, Be thou cast into the depths of the sea, and it shall be done"—the sole secret of success, a will that knows no "perhaps," and a faith whose confidence no temporary failure can shake.

This theory of the action of a new consciousness, framed out of the intelligences of those present at the experiment, has been many times put forward, to be as often upset by some fact which it is not sufficient to explain. It is the fate of theories. All gravitate to the same grave, until the time comes and the man, who explains, in the light of accumulated facts, by severe process of deductive logic, what insufficient knowledge has only blundered over.

Perhaps the greatest light will be shed on these obscure phenomena by the study of mesmerism. The passive state in which the Psychic is thrown before any phenomena are produced may be regarded by some as a state of auto-mesmerism, during which his liberated spirit displays some of the strange phenomena of clairvoyance, prevision, introvision, and the like, which successful mesmerists study in their "subjects." The trance-state, during which the best phenomena are observed, is one known to mesmerists by the name of *ecstasis*, and many remarkable facts are recorded respecting it, as, for instance, in a valuable work on the subject by Professor Gregory, F.R.S.E., entitled *Animal Magnetism*. This has been lately republished by Mr. Harrison (38, Great Russell Street), and is an excellent introduction to the study of the phenomena now under notice.

Indeed the whole subject of the trans-corporeal action of the human spirit—its power of making its presence felt far away from its bodily prison-house under the influence of strong emotion; its sympathies and antipathies; its strange power of mind-reading and transfusion of thought, under certain circumstances and in certain states;—are all points to be cleared up by the student of these phenomena before he ought to venture far into the domain of theory. Professor Barrett very properly said, in the course of a letter to *The Times*, when the Slade prosecution was before the public: "I am inclined to believe that other mental phenomena—such, for example, as the possibility of the action of one mind upon another, across space, without the intervention of the senses—demand a prior investigation." He had previously recommended the study of mesmerism; and he might have added that the whole subject of Psychology in its various branches, respecting which so little is now known, should receive careful attention in the light of knowledge which ancient students possessed. It is thus that the gates will be opened, after prolonged and patient investigation and study.

But when all this has been admitted, and when these theorisers have said their say, there remains, it must be confessed, a numerous, compact, and firm body of observers who correlate these phenomena with others called spiritual, and refer them to the action of disembodied human spirits. These are the Spiritualists *pur sang*. They cut the knot of every difficulty with an all-sufficient knife; and, starting with a tremendous postulate, account for everything on comprehensive principles. They say, in effect, that the pretensions which, it must be conceded, are invariably put forward by the intelligent operator are such as they see no reason to reject. They ask, with considerable cogency, what ground the theorist has for rejecting a hypothesis which has the merit of being consistently put forward by the Invisible Intelligence; and why this Intelligence, being interrogated, should invariably return an answer identifying itself with the spirit of a departed human being, if it be, indeed, as alleged, only the liberated spirit of the Psychic? They propound, indeed, several difficulties which are somewhat staggering to the theorists who maintain the action of the spirit of the Psychic as the sole and sufficient cause; and—with a faith which, if it cannot move mountains, has apparently no difficulty in swallowing them—all to them is plain and simple. The world of spirit, they say, is all around us, only a crass materialism has so blinded our eyes that we can no longer discern it, save in those comparatively rare cases where the gulf is bridged by Psychic power. The various Biblical records, which I need not quote, of the intervention of spirit on the material plane, fortify them in their faith, which, they allege, has the venerable prescription of *semper, ubique, et ab omnibus* (who, at least, have not wilfully closed their spiritual eyes, or become spiritually blind by inheritance of defective spiritual sense). These claim kinship, too, with the great Eastern schools of thought whose adepts can demonstrate at will what the Western Psychic only fitfully evokes. They contend that what strikes the English mind as portentously incredible is matter of every-day experience to the spiritually-cultured Eastern; as it has been to all who have striven to obey the maxim, *Know thyself.*

Between these various theories—and their ramifications are far wider than I have thought it necessary to indicate—the candid reader may be left to choose, unless, indeed, he be made in that rare and robust mould which is content with facts and facts only, satisfied with accumulating and preserving them, and willing to leave theory to the day when sufficient material shall have been accumulated to lift a deduction out of the mists of mere speculation.

Deductions, Explanations, and Theories. 147

In concluding, I am bold to reiterate what I said at starting. I have no controversial end in view, else my tone had been other than it has been. I have neither the wish nor the power to force unwelcome truth on unwilling minds. My aim has been to record facts for such as will value them. I have but enumerated certain theories, without any desire—at this juncture, and in this volume—to advocate any of them. In the words of Professor Gregory—writing, I am rejoiced to think, about a subject then sneered at, but now generally accepted—"My object has not been to explain the facts I have described, but rather to show that a large number of facts exist which require explanation, but which can never be explained unless we study them. I am quite content that any theoretical suggestions I have made should be thrown aside as quite unimportant, provided the facts be attended to, because I consider it too early for a comprehensive theory, and because I believe the facts are as yet but very partially known."—*Animal Magnetism*, p. 252.

APPENDIX.

SINCE writing the body of this volume, two or three facts have come under my notice which I take this means of noticing.

1. Henry Slade, being then resident at Berlin, was visited by the Court Conjurer and Prestidigitator to the Emperor of Germany, Samuel Bellachini, No. 14 Grossbaron-strasse, who subsequently made affidavit before a public notary, Gustav Haagen, in the following terms:—

Executed at Berlin on the sixth of December, one thousand eight hundred and seventy-seven, and entered in the Notary's register under the number four hundred and eighty-two, for the year eighteen hundred and seventy-seven.
Signed and officially stamped.

GUSTAV HAAGEN, *Counsellor and Notary.*

I hereby declare it to be a rash action to give decisive judgment upon the objective medial performance of the American medium, Mr. Henry Slade, after only one sitting, and the observations so made.

After I had, at the wish of several highly-esteemed gentlemen of rank and position, and also for my own interest, tested the physical mediumship of Mr. Slade in a series of sittings by full daylight, as well as in the evening, in his bedroom, I must, for the sake of truth, hereby certify that the phenomenal occurrences with Mr. Slade, have been thoroughly examined by me, with the minutest observation and investigation of his surroundings, including the table, and that I have *not in the smallest instance* found anything to be produced by means of prestidigitative manifestations, or by mechanical apparatus, and that any explanation of the experiments which took place *under the circumstances and conditions then obtaining*, by any reference to prestidigitation, *to be absolutely impossible.*

It must rest with such men of science as Crookes and Wallace, in London; Perty, in Berne; Boutlerof, in St. Petersburg, to search for the explanation of this phenomenal power, and to prove its reality. I declare, moreover, the published opinions of laymen, as to the "how" of this subject to be premature, and according to *my* view and experience, false and one-sided. This, my declaration, is signed and executed before a notary and witnesses.

(Signed)   SAMUEL BELLACHINI.

Berlin, 6th December, 1877.

2. Henry Slade having proceeded to St. Petersburg in order to fulfil his engagement with M. Aksakof and Professor Boutlerof, and to present the phenomenon of Psychography to the scrutiny of a committee of scientific experts, has had a series of successful sittings, in the course of which writing has been obtained in the Russian language. At one recent sitting writing in six different languages was obtained on a single slate.

On Wednesday, Feb. 20, accompanied by M. Aksakof and Professor Boutlerof, Slade had a most successful sitting with the Grand Duke Constantine, who received them cordially, and himself obtained writing on a new slate held by himself alone.

3. The Rev. Thomas Colley thus testifies, under date January 17, 1878 :—

This afternoon I had a sitting with Dr. Monck of a somewhat unique character. I had purchased this morning a transparent drawing-slate; and, taking out one of the pictures, I wrote my name on the edge of it, with a request that it and the five objects of the composite sketch might be traced on the rough side of the ground glass. Not letting Dr. Monck know what I had done, I placed the marked picture between the five others—three before it and the glass, and two behind it and the back of the frame. Then, taking it with me, and not allowing him once to touch it, and scarcely to see it, as I took it from the side-pocket of my coat, I placed it, with a lead pencil, beneath the easy chair in which Dr. Monck was sitting (around the lower part of which I had placed a carriage-rug, to make a sort of camera-obscura), and held his hands, placing my feet on his feet, and my knees to his knees, as I sat facing him.

Under these conditions, not asking orally for what I desired to be done, or intimating in any way to Dr. Monck the nature or particulars of the experiment I was making, "Samuel" took momentary control, and told me he had accomplished the matter, affirming that not only had he drawn the marked picture and traced my autograph, but also that he had written on the back of the picture these words, "Take this to Serjeant Cox," particularly calling my attention at the time to the fact that he had, in a peculiar way, abbreviated the word Serjeant.

Control then instantly passed off; and not relinquishing Dr. Monck's hands, or removing my feet from his, with partially disengaged fingers I took the transparent slate as it was pushed up from under the chair, and found a picture traced on the glass, and my name over, written in my own characters. But this did not agree with the picture next the glass; it manifestly was a copy of the drawing I had marked and placed between the others. This was verified later on in the day, for, taking the transparent slate with me, I went straight to the adjourned debate on Psychography at the Psychological Society, and handed it to the President (Serjeant Cox), who publicly opened it and found the marked picture where I had originally placed it—the fourth from the glass and third from the back; and on taking it out and placing it under the ground glass, the strongly-outlined lead-pencil sketch on this latter was found accurately to agree with the drawing beneath. There also, by the learned President (for I had for the moment forgotten the circumstance), the writing on the body of the paper was found, referring to him: "Take this to Ser. Cox."

STANDARD BOOKS
ON
SPIRITUALISM, MESMERISM, PSCYHOLOGY, ANTHROPOLOGY,
AND KINDRED SUBJECTS,
PUBLISHED BY W. H. HARRISON,
38 GREAT RUSSELL STREET, LONDON, W.C.

Lists of the Books are Advertised in every Number of the *The Spiritualist* Newspaper.

W. H. Harrison's Publications may be obtained from Messrs. Colby & Rich, 9 Montgomery Place, Boston, United States; and from Mr. W. H. Terry, 84 Russell St. South, Melbourne, Australia.

"THE SPIRITUALIST" NEWSPAPER:

A Record of the Progress of the Science and Ethics of Spiritualism.

PUBLISHED WEEKLY, PRICE TWOPENCE.
Established in 1869.

The Spiritualist, published weekly, is the oldest Newspaper connected with the movement in the United Kingdom, and is the recognised organ of educated Spiritualists in all the English-speaking countries throughout the Globe. It also has an influential body of readers on the Continent of Europe.

The Contributors to its pages comprise the leading and more experienced Spiritualists, including many eminent in the ranks of Literature, Art, Science, and the Nobility of Europe. Among those who have published their names in connection with their communications in its columns are Mr. C. F. Varley, C.E., F.R.S.; Mr William Crookes, F.R.S., Editor of the *Quarterly Journal of Science* (who admits the reality of the phenomena, but has, up to the present time, expressed no decided opinion as to their cause); Mr. Alfred R. Wallace, President of the Biological Section of the British Association for the Advancement of Science (1876); Prince Emile de Sayn-Wittgenstein (Wiesbaden); the Right Hon. the Countess of Caithness; His Imperial Highness Nicholas of Russia (Duke of Leuchtenberg); Mr. H. G. Atkinson, F.G.S.; The Lord Lindsay; the Hon. Robert Dale Owen, formerly American Minister

[ADVERTISEMENTS.]
W. H. HARRISON'S PUBLICATIONS.

at the Court of Naples; Baron Dirckinck-Holmfield (Holstein); Mr. Gerald Massey; Le Comte de Bullet; the Hon. J. L. O'Sullivan, formerly American Minister at the Court of Portugal; Mr. C. C. Massey, Barrister-at-Law; Mr. George C. Joad; Dr. Robert Wyld; Mr. T. P. Barkas, F.G.S.; Mr. Serjeant Cox, President of the Psychological Society of Great Britain; Mr. Alexander Calder, President of the British National Association of Spiritualists; the Rev. J. Tyerman (Australia); Mr. Epes Sargent (Boston, U.S.); Sir Charles Isham, Bart.; Mrs. Ross-Church (Florence Marryat); Mrs. Makdougall Gregory; the Hon. Alexandre Aksakof, Russian Imperial Councillor, and Chevalier of the Order of St. Stanislas (St. Petersburg); the Baroness Adelma Von Vay (Austria); Mr. H. M. Dunphy, Barrister-at-Law; Mr. C. Carter Blake, Doc. Sci., Lecturer on Comparative Anatomy at Westminster Hospital; Mr. Stanhope Templeman Speer, M.D. (Edin.); Mr. J. C. Luxmoore; Mr. John E. Purdon, M.B. (India); Mrs. Honywood; Mr. Benjamin Coleman; Mr. Charles Blackburn; Mr. St. George W. Stock, B.A. (Oxon); Mr. James Wason; Mr. N. Fabyan Dawe; Herr Christian Reimers; Mr. Wm. White (author of the "Life of Swedenborg"); Mr. J. M. Gully, M.D.; the Rev. C. Maurice Davies, D.D., author of "Unorthodox London"; Mr. S. C. Hall, F.S.A.; Mrs. S. C. Hall; Mr. William Newton, F.R.G.S.; Mr. H. D. Jencken, M.R.I., Barrister-at-Law; Mr. Algernon Joy, M.Inst.C.E.; Mr. D. H. Wilson, M.A., LL.M.; Mr. C. Constant (Smyrna); Mrs. F. A. Nosworthy; Mr. Wm. Oxley; Miss Kislingbury; Miss A. Blackwell (Paris); Mrs. F. Showers; Mr. J. N. T. Martheze; Mr. J. M. Peebles (United States); Mr. W. Lindesay Richardson, M.D. (Australia); Baboo Peary Chand Mittra (Calcutta); Mr. Eugene Crowell, M.D. (New York); and many other ladies and gentlemen.

Annual subscription to residents in the United Kingdom, 10s. 10d.; in the United States and Australia, 13s., post free.

The Spiritualist is regularly on sale at the following places:—London: 11 Ave Maria Lane, St. Paul's Churchyard, E.C. Paris: Kiosque, 246 Boulevard des Capucines, and 7 Rue de Lille. Leipzig: 2 Lindenstrasse. Florence: Signor G. Parisi, Via della Maltonaia. Rome: Signor Bocca, Libraio, Via del Corso. Naples: British Reading Rooms, 267 Riviera di Chiaja, opposite the Villa Nazionale. Liege: 37 Rue Florimont. Buda-Pesth: Josefstaadt Erzherzog, 23 Alexander Gasse. Melbourne: 96 Russell Street. Shanghai: Messrs. Kelly & Co. New York: Harvard Rooms, Forty-second Street and Sixth Avenue.

[ADVERTISEMENTS.]

W. H. HARRISON'S PUBLICATIONS.

Boston, U.S.: 9 Montgomery Place, and 18 Exchange Street. Chicago: *Religio-Philosophical Journal* Office. Memphis, U.S.: 225 Union Street. San Francisco: 319 Kearney Street. Philadelphia: 918 Spring Garden Street. Washington: No. 1010 Seventh Street.

All communications on the business of *The Spiritualist* should be addressed to W. H. Harrison, *Spiritualist* Newspaper Branch Office, 38 Great Russell St., London, W.C.

MESMERISM AND ITS PHENOMENA,

OR

ANIMAL MAGNETISM,

By the late WM. GREGORY, M.D., F.R.S.E., Professor of Chemistry at Edinburgh University.

Dedicated by the Author by Permission to His Grace George Douglas-Campbell, Duke of Argyll.

This second and slightly revised and abridged edition, is for its quality and size the cheapest large work ever published in England in connection with Spiritualism.

(THE CHIEF STANDARD WORK ON MESMERISM.)

Just Published, price 5s., or 5s. 6d. post free: or five copies post free for 21s. Copies may also be had bound in half calf, with marbled edges, price 8s. 6d. per volume, post free.

CONTENTS.

CHAPTER I.—First Effects Produced by Mesmerism—Sensations—Process for Causing Mesmeric Sleep—The Sleep or Mesmeric State—It Occurs Spontaneously in Sleep-Walkers—Phenomena of the Sleep—Divided Conciousness—Senses Affected—Insensibility to Pain.

CHAPTER II.—Control Exercised by the Operator over the Subject in Various Ways—Striking Expression of Feelings in the Look and Gesture—Effect of Music—Truthfulness of the Sleeper—Various Degrees of Susceptibility—Sleep Caused by Silent Will, and at a Distance—Attraction Towards the Operator—Effect in the Waking State of Commands Given in the Sleep.

CHAPTER III.—Sympathy—Community of Sensations; of Emotions—Danger of Rash Experiments—Public Exhibitions of Doubtful Advantage—Sympathy with the Bystanders—Thought-Reading—Sources of Error—Medical Intuition—Sympathetic Warnings—Sympathies and Antipathies—Existence of a Peculiar Force or Influence.

CHAPTER IV.—Direct Clairvoyance or Lucid Vision, without the Eyes—Vision of Near Objects: through

[ADVERTISEMENTS.]
W. H. HARRISON'S PUBLICATIONS.

Opaque Bodies: at a Distance—Sympathy and Clairvoyance in Regard to Absent Persons—Retrovision—Introvision.

CHAPTER V.—Lucid Prevision—Duration of Sleep, &c., Predicted—Prediction of Changes in the Health or State of the Seer—Prediction of Accidents, and of Events Affecting Others—Spontaneous Clairvoyance—Striking Case of it—Spontaneous Retrovision and Prevision—Peculiarities of Speech and of Consciousness in Mesmerised Persons—Transference of Senses and of Pain.

CHAPTER VI.—Mesmerism, Electro-Biology, Electro-Psychology and Hypnotism, essentially the same—Phenomena of Suggestions in the Conscious or Waking State—Dr. Darling's Method and its Effects—Mr. Lewis's Method and its Results—The Impressible State—Control Exercised by the Operator—Gazing—Mr. Braid's Hypnotism—The Author's Experience—Importance of Perseverance—The Subject must be Studied.

CHAPTER VII.—Trance, Natural and Accidental; Mesmeric—Trance Produced at Will by the Subjects—Colonel Townsend—Fakeers—Extasis—Extatics not all Impostors—Luminous Emanations—Extasis often Predicted—M. Cahagnet's Extatics—Visions of the Spiritual World.

CHAPTER VIII.—Phreno-Mesmerism—Progress of Phrenology—Effects of Touching the Head in the Sleep—Variety in the Phenomena—Suggestion—Sympathy—There are Cases in which these Act, and others in which they do not Act—Phenomena Described—The Lower Animals Susceptible of Mesmerism—Fascination Among Animals—Instinct—Sympathy of Animals—Snail Telegraph Founded on It.

CHAPTER IX.—Action of Magnets, Crystals, &c., on the Human Frame—Researches of Reichenbach—His Odyle is Identical with the Mesmeric Fluid of Mesmer, or with the Influence which Causes the Mesmeric Phenomena—Odylic or Mesmeric Light—Aurora Borealis Artificially Produced—Mesmerised Water—Useful Applications of Mesmerism—Physiological, Therapeutical, &c.—Treatment of Insanity, Magic, Divination, Witchcraft, &c., explained by Mesmerism, and Traced to Natural Causes—Apparitions—Second Sight is Waking Clairvoyance—Predictions of Various Kinds.

CHAPTER X.—An Explanation of the Phenomena Attempted or Suggested—A Force (Odyle) Universally Diffused, Certainly Exists, and is Probably the Medium of Sympathy and Lucid Vision—Its Characters—Difficulties of the Subject—Effects of Odyle—Somnambulism—Suggestion, Sympathy—Thought-Reading—Lucid Vision—Odylic Emanations—Odylic Traces followed up by Lucid

[ADVERTISEMENTS.]

W. H. HARRISON'S PUBLICATIONS.

Subjects—Magic and Witchcraft—The Magic Crystal, and Mirror, &c., Induce Walking Clairvoyance—Universal Sympathy—Lucid Perception of the Future.

CHAPTER XI.—Interest Felt in Mesmerism by Men of Science—Due Limits of Scientific Caution—Practical Hints—Conditions of Success in Experiments—Cause of Failure—Mesmerism a Serious Thing—Cautions to the Student—Opposition to be Expected.

CHAPTER XII.—Phenomena Observed in the Conscious or Waking State—Effects of Suggestion on Persons in an Impressible State—Mr. Lewis's Experiments With and Without Suggestion—Cases—Dr. Darling's Experiments—Cases—Conscious or Waking Clairvoyance, Produced by Passes, or by Concentration—Major Buckley's Method—Cases—The Magic Crystal Induces Waking Lucidity, when Gazed at—Cases—Magic Mirror—Mesmerised Water—Egyptian Magic.

CHAPTER XIII.—Production of the Mesmeric Sleep—Cases—Eight out of Nine Persons Recently Tried by the Author Thrown into Mesmeric Sleep—Sleep Produced without the Knowledge of the Subject—Suggestion in the Sleep—Phreno-Mesmerism in the Sleep—Sympathetic Clairvoyance in the Sleep—Cases—Perception of Time—Cases; Sir J. Franklin; Major Buckley's Case of Retrovision.

CHAPTER XIV.—Direct Clairvoyance—Cases—Travelling Clairvoyance—Cases—Singular Visions of Mr. D.—Letters of Two Clergymen, with Cases—Clairvoyance of Alexis—Other Cases.

CHAPTER XV.—Trance—Extasis—Cases—Spontaneous Mesmeric Phenomena—Apparitions—Predictions.

CHAPTER XVI.—Curative Agency of Mesmerism—Concluding Remarks, and Summary.

SPIRIT PEOPLE:

A scientifically accurate description of Manifestations recently produced by Spirits, and

SIMULTANEOUSLY WITNESSED BY THE AUTHOR AND OTHER OBSERVERS IN LONDON.

By WILLIAM H. HARRISON.

Limp Cloth, red edges. Price 1s.; post free 1s. 1d.

OPINIONS OF THE PRESS.

"As a dispassionate scientific man, he appears to have investigated the subject without pre-conceived ideas, and the result of his examination has been to identify his opinions with those of Messrs. Varley,

[ADVERTISEMENTS.]

W. H. HARRISON'S PUBLICATIONS.

Crookes, & Wallace, in favour not only of the absolute reality of the phenomena, but also of the genuineness of the communications alleged to be given by the spirits of the departed."—*Public Opinion.*

"At the outset of his booklet Mr. Harrison disclaims any intention of proselytising or forcing his opinion down non-Spiritualistic throats, and it is only fair to admit that the succeeding pages are remarkably free from argument and deduction, albeit bristling with assertions of the most dumbfounding nature."—London *Figaro.*

"He neither theorises nor dogmatises, nor attempts to make converts to his views. He states occurrences and events, or what he believes did really happen, in a remarkably clear and narrative style, without any attempt at advocacy or argument."—*South Wales Daily News.*

Just Published, Price Seven Shillings and Sixpence, Crown 8vo., Richly Gilt,

THE LAZY LAYS,
AND PROSE IMAGININGS.
By WILLIAM H. HARRISON.

An Elegant and Amusing Gift-Book of Poetical and Prose Writings, Grave and Gay.

The gilt device on the cover designed by Florence Claxton and the Author.

CONTENTS.

Part I.—*Miscellaneous Poems and Prose Writings.*

1. The Lay of the Lazy Author.—2. The Song of the Newspaper Editor.—3. The Song of the Pawnbroker.—4. The Castle.—5. The Lay of the Fat Man.—6. The Poetry of Science.—7. How Hadji Al Shacabac was Photographed (a letter from Hadji Al Shacabac, a gentleman who visited London on business connected with a Turkish Loan, to Ali Mustapha Ben Buckram, Chief of the College of Howling Dervishes at Constantinople).—8. The Lay of the Broad-Brimmed Hat.—9. St. Bride's Bay.—10. The Lay of the Market Gardener.—11. "Fast Falls the Eventide."—12. Our Raven.—13. Materialistic Religion.—14. The Lay of the Photographer.—15. How to Double the Utility of the Printing Press.—16. The Song of the Mother-in-Law.—17. *Wirbel-bewegung.*—18. "Poor Old Joe!"—19. The Human Hive.—20. The Lay of the Mace-Bearers.—21. A Love Song.—22. A Vision.—23. "Under the Limes."—24. The Angel of Silence.

Part II.—*The Wobblejaw Ballads, by Anthony Wobblejaws.*

25. The Public Analyst.—26. General Grant's Reception at Folkestone.—27. The Rifle Corps.—28. Tony's Lament. 29. The July Bug.—30. The Converted Carman.

[ADVERTISEMENTS.]

W. H. HARRISON'S PUBLICATIONS.

OPINIONS OF THE PRESS.

From the *Morning Post*.

The *Morning Post*, which strongly recommends the book in a review nearly a column long, says:—"Comic literature which honestly deserves the epithet seems to be rapidly becoming a thing of the past; consequently any writer who, like Mr. Harrison, exhibits a genuine vein of humour, deserves the praise of all who are not too stupid to enjoy an innocent laugh. Not that his muse restricts herself only to such lighter utterances; on the contrary, some of his poems touch on the deepest and most sacred feelings of our common humanity. . . . The unfortunate Hadji's narrative of his adventures amongst the magicians of Whitechapel is quite one of the funniest things that has been published for years. . . . The book contains quite enough to ensure it a welcome from which its tasteful appearance will not detract." The *Morning Post* says of the "Wobblejaw Ballads":—"No one can help laughing at them."

From the *Court Journal*.

"All are of marked ability. . . . Occasionally we find verse of great beauty, showing that the author possesses the pure poetic gift."

From the *Graphic*.

"Those who can appreciate genuine, unforced humour should not fail to read 'The Lazy Lays and Prose Imaginings.' Written, printed, published, and reviewed by William H. Harrison (38 Great Russell Street). Both the verses and the short essays are really funny, and in some of the latter there is a vein of genial satire which adds piquancy to the fun."

From *Public Opinion*.

"A volume of remarkably good verse. . . . Some of the metrical legends remind us of the wild chants that used to be sung at the meetings of the Cannibal Club, some ten or fifteen years ago. Mr. Harrison, however, knows where to plant his fun; and an accurate scientific mind like his can make jokes with success. . . . To all who wish to read a pleasant volume magnificently got up as a gift-book, we commend 'The Lazy Lays.'"

From the *Bookseller*.

"An odd but most entertaining assortment of quaint and humorous fancies, some in verse and others in prose, and all written with a fluent and not ungraceful pen. The vein of humour which permeates them is genuine, rich, and original, and not at all ill-natured."

From *Nature*.

"Scientific men and matters are in one or two cases alluded to, and the imprint bears that the work is published 'A.D. 1877 (popular chronology); A.M. 5877 (Torquemada); A.M. 50,800,077 (Huxley).' We believe that our readers may derive a little amusement from a perusal of the volume."

From the *British Journal of Photography*.

"'The Lazy Lays' include many admirable pieces, some of which are in verse and others in prose, some scientific, others social, but all of them excellent. . . . 'The Lazy Lays' will make excellent and amusing reading for an occasional spare half-hour. . . . They contain nothing unrefined or in bad taste."

From the *Dublin University Magazine*.

"How Hadji Al Shacabac, an amiable Turk, was photographed, is well done. . . . Bound in a cover of somewhat powerful design."

From the *Photographic News*.

"Mr. W. H. Harrison, a gentleman whose name is familiar in connection with photographic and other scientific literature, has considerable facility of versification, and deals, in pleasant and humorous mood, with many scientific follies which are better laughed down than gravely disputed."

[ADVERTISEMENTS.]

W. H. HARRISON'S PUBLICATIONS.

From the *Scotsman.*

"In Mr. W. H. Harrison's 'Lazy Lays and Prose Imaginings' there is a good deal of broad humour and satiric power, with a due foundation of solid sense."

From the *Bradford Daily Chronicle.*

"Good poetical diction is displayed. Mr. Harrison has produced a most welcome book. . . . 'How Hadji Al Shacabac was Photographed,' will be sure to make every reader roar with laughter."

From the *Dundee Daily Advertiser.*

"With such a free and easy author it is naturally to be expected that his subjects should bear some trace of this peculiar idiosyncrasy; and indeed they are as free and easy as himself. . . . The poems are all characterised by smoothness and rhythmical swing. . . . The work is very elaborately bound in cloth and gilt. . . . A gorgeous design upon the cover. . . . If our readers wish to encourage laziness, they have a most deserving object in a very clever and versatile member of the order."

From the *Liverpool Daily Courier.*

"In his handsomely-bound and griffin-guarded 'Lazy Lays,' Mr. William H. Harrison provides a gift-book elegant in its appearance and entertaining in its contents. . . . The author is imbued with the true spirit of humour, and amuses all while offending none."

From the *Western Daily Press* (Bristol).

"A volume from the versatile pen of Mr. W. H. Harrison, a well-known contributor to the London and provincial press, and editor of the *Spiritualist*. . . . Many of the humorous poems remind us of the 'Ingoldsby Legends.' 'The Lay of the Photographer,' 'The Lay of the Macebearers,' and some of 'The Wobblejaw Ballads' would not have been unworthy of Barham himself. Some of the shorter poems are exquisite, and there pervade the whole a religious sentiment and poetic feeling which will make them acceptable to most readers."

From the daily *Northern Whig* (Belfast).

"The finest thing in the book is 'How Hadji Al Shacabac was Photographed.' It is an admirable addition to our not too extensive comic literature. The story is one of which extracts could not give an adequate idea; it is intensely humorous. . . . Those who wish to obtain a handsome gift-book of an amusing nature, will find what they want in 'The Lazy Lays.'"

From the *Kensington News.*

It is "after the manner of Barham, Hood, Mark Twain, or any of those merry souls who do quite as much good in their day and generation as the authors of the most serious works."

From the *Malvern News.*

"It is in itself a work of itself—original, and a cast of its author's mind. It is a work of great power and beauty; full of lively imaginings and bold outspoken thoughts, abounding in tenderness and pathos; sparkling with wit and humour; and one that may be read many times over. . . . The get-up of the book is very handsome."

From the *Folkestone News.*

"A number of clever sketches and poems, among the latter being a series of papers entitled 'The Wobblejaw Ballads,' which appeared in the columns of this paper a short time ago, and which created such a *furore* at the time." [*N.B.—An irate member of the Town Council officially called the attention of the Mayor and Corporation of Folkestone to the burlesques in the "Wobblejaw Ballads;" but the members assembled laughed at the matter, and proceeded to the next business. The Mayor said that he did not mind them.*] . . . "It contains some very choice poems and prose essays, is bound in cloth richly gilt, and has an original design of no ordinary merit on the cover."

[ADVERTISEMENTS.]

W. H. HARRISON'S PUBLICATIONS.

Price 5s., cloth, red edges.

PSYCHOGRAPHY.
By M. A. OXON.

SYNOPSIS OF CONTENTS.

LIST OF WORKS BEARING ON THE SUBJECT.
PREFACE.
INTRODUCTION.
PSYCHOGRAPHY IN THE PAST: Guldenstubbé—Crookes.
PERSONAL EXPERIENCES IN PRIVATE, AND WITH PUBLIC PSYCHICS.

GENERAL CORROBORATIVE EVIDENCE.

I. That Attested by the Senses—
   1. *Of Sight.*
      Evidence of Mr. E. T. Bennett.
        ,,   a Malvern Reporter.
        ,,   Mr. James Burns.
        ,,   Mr. H. D. Jencken.
   2. *Of Hearing.*
      Evidence of Mr. Serjeant Cox.
        ,,   Mr. George King.
        ,,   Mr. Hensleigh Wedgwood.
        ,,   Miss * * * *
        ,,   Canon Mouls.
        ,,   Baroness Von Vay.
        ,,   G. H. Adshead.
        ,,   W. P. Adshead.
        ,,   E. H. Valter.
        ,,   J. L. O'Sullivan.
        ,,   Epes Sargent.
        ,,   James O. Sargent.
        ,,   John Wetherbee.
        ,,   H. B. Storer.
        ,,   C. A. Greenleaf.
        ,,   Public Committee with Watkins.

II. From the Writing of Languages Unknown to the Psychic.
   Ancient Greek—Evidence of Hon. R. Dale Owen and Mr. Blackburn. (Slade.)
   Dutch, German, French, Spanish, Portuguese. (Slade.)
   Russian—Evidence of Madame Blavatsky. (Watkins.)
   Romaic—Evidence of T. T. Timayenis. (Watkins.)
   Chinese. (Watkins.)

[ADVERTISEMENTS.]
W. H. HARRISON'S PUBLICATIONS.

III. From Special Tests which Preclude Previous Preparation of the Writing.
    Psychics and Conjurers Contrasted.
    Slade before the Research Committee of the British National Association of Spiritualists.
    Slade Tested by C. Carter Blake, Doc. Sci.
    Evidence of Rev. J. Page Hopps. (Slade.)
    ,,   W. H. Harrison. (Slade.)
    ,,   J. Seaman. (Slade.)
    Writing within Slates securely screwed together.
    Evidence of Mrs. Andrews and J. Mould.
    Dictation of Words at the Time of the Experiment.
    Evidence of A. R. Wallace, F.R.G.S.
        ,,   Hensleigh Wedgwood, J.P.
        ,,   Rev. Thomas Colley.
        ,,   W. Oxley.
        ,,   George Wyld, M.D.
        ,,   Miss Kislingbury.
    Writing in Answer to Questions Inside a Closed Box.
    Evidence of Messrs. Adshead.
    Statement of Circumstances under which Experiments with F. W. Monck were conducted at Keighley.
    Writing on Glass Coated with White Paint.
    Evidence of Benjamin Coleman.
Letters addressed to *The Times* on the Subject of the Prosecution of Henry Slade by Messrs. Joy, Joad, and Professor Barrett, F.R.S.E.
Evidence of W. H. Harrison, Editor of *The Spiritualist*.

SUMMARY OF FACTS NARRATED.

    DEDUCTIONS, EXPLANATIONS, AND THEORIES.
The Nature of the Force: Its Mode of Operation.
    Evidence of C. Carter Blake, Doc. Sci., and Conrad Cooke, C.E.
Detonating Noises in Connection with it.
    Evidence of Hensleigh Wedgwood, J. Page Hopps, Thomas Colley.
Method of Direction of the Force.
    Dr. Collyer's Theory.
    Dr. George Wyld's Theory.
    The Occultist's Theory.
    The Spiritualist's Theory.

APPENDIX.
    The Court Conjurer of Berlin on Slade.
    Slade with the Grand Duke Constantine.
    Recent Experiment with Monck.

[ADVERTISEMENTS.]
W. H. HARRISON'S PUBLICATIONS.

Price 5s., richly gilt,

"RIFTS IN THE VEIL."

A collection of choice poems and prose essays given through mediumship, also of articles and poems written by Spiritualists. A useful book to place in public libraries, and to present or lend to those who are unacquainted with Spiritualism.

CONTENTS.

1. Introduction : The Philosophy of Inspiration.
2. "O! Beautiful White Mother Death." Given through the trance-mediumship of Cora L. V. Tappan-Richmond.
3. The Apparition of Sengireef. By Sophie Aksakof.
4. The Translation of Shelley to the Higher Life. Given through the trance-mediumship of T. L. Harris.
5. Gone Home. Given through the trance-mediumship of Lizzie Doten.
6. The Birth of the Spirit. Given through the trance-mediumship of Cora L. V. Tappan-Richmond.
7. Angel Guarded.
8. An Alleged Post-Mortem Work by Charles Dickens. How the writings were produced: The Magnificent Egotist, Sapsea: Mr. Stollop Reveals a Secret : A Majestic Mind Severely Tried : Dwellers in Cloisterham: Mr. Peter Peckcraft and Miss Keep : Critical Comments.
9. The Spider of the Period. By Georgina Weldon (Miss Treherne) and Mrs. ———.
10. Margery Miller. Given through the trance-mediumship of Lizzie Doten.
11. Ode by "Adamanta."
12. Swedenborg on Men and Women. By William White, author of *The Life of Swedenborg*.
13. Resurgam. By Caroline A. Burke.
14. Abnormal Spectres of Wolves, Dogs, and other Animals. By Emile, Prince of Wittgenstein.
15. To you who Loved Me. By Florence Marryat.
16. Desolation. By Caroline A. Burke.
17. Truth. Given through the mediumship of "M.A., Oxon."
18. Thy Love. By Florence Marryat.
19. Haunting Spirits. By the Baroness Adelma Von Vay (Countess Würmbrand).
20. Fashionable Grief for the Departed.
21. The Brown Lady of Rainham. By Lucia C. Stone.
22. A Vision of Death. By Caroline A. Burke.

[ADVERTISEMENTS.]

W. H. HARRISON'S PUBLICATIONS.

23. A Story of a Haunted House. By F. J. Theobald.
24. "Love the Truth and Peace." By the Rev. C. Maurice Davies, D.D.
25. The Ends, Aims, and Uses of Modern Spiritualism. By Louisa Lowe.
26. De Profundis. By Anna Blackwell.
27. Ancient Thought and Modern Spiritualism. By C. Carter Blake, Doc. Sci., Lecturer on Comparative Anatomy at Westminster Hospital.
28. Die Sehnsucht. Translated by Emily Kislingbury, from the German of Schiller.
29. The Relation of Spiritualism to Orthodox Christianity. Given through the mediumship of "M.A., Oxon."
30. A *Seance* in the Sunshine. By the Rev. C. Maurice Davies, D.D.
31. "My Saint." By Florence Marryat.
32. The Death-beds of Spiritualists. By Epes Sargent.
33. The Touch of a Vanished Hand. By the Rev. C. Maurice Davies, D.D.
34. Death. By Caroline A. Burke.
35. The Spirit Creed. Through the mediumship of "M.A., Oxon."
36. The Angel of Silence. By W. H. Harrison.
37. The Prediction. By Alice Worthington (Ennesfallen).
38. Longfellow's Position in Relation to Spiritualism.
39. Spiritual Manifestations among the Fakirs in India. By Dr. Maximilian Perty, Professor of Natural Philosophy, Berne; translated from *Psychic Studies* (Leipzig) by Emily Kislingbury.
40. The Poetry of Science. By W. H. Harrison.
41. Meditation and the Voice of Conscience. By Alex. Calder.
42. Dirge. By Mrs. Eric Baker.
43. Epigrams. By Gerald Massey.
44. Some of the Difficulties of the Clergy in Relation to Spiritualism. By Lisette Makdougall Gregory.
45. Immortality. By Alfred Russel Wallace, F.R.G.S.
46. A Child's Prayer. By Gerald Massey.

W. H. HARRISON, 38 Great Russell-street, W.C.

www.ingramcontent.com/pod-product-compliance
Lightning Source LLC
Chambersburg PA
CBHW030258170426
43202CB00009B/789